NORTH WEST ENGLAND

Edited by Allison Dowse

First published in Great Britain in 2003 by
YOUNG WRITERS
Remus House,
Coltsfoot Drive,
Peterborough, PE2 9JX
Telephone (01733) 890066

All Rights Reserved

Copyright Contributors 2003

HB ISBN 1 84460 092 0
SB ISBN 1 84460 093 9

FOREWORD

Young Writers was established in 1991 as a foundation for promoting the reading and writing of poetry amongst children and young adults. Today it continues this quest and proceeds to nurture and guide the writing talents of today's youth.

From this year's competition Young Writers is proud to present a showcase of the best poetic talent from across the UK. Each hand-picked poem has been carefully chosen from over 66,000 'Hullabaloo!' entries to be published in this, our eleventh primary school series.

This year in particular we have been wholeheartedly impressed with the quality of entries received. The thought, effort, imagination and hard work put into each poem impressed us all and once again the task of editing was a difficult but enjoyable experience.

We hope you are as pleased as we are with the final selection and that you and your family will continue to be entertained with *Hullabaloo! North West England* for many years to come.

CONTENTS

Cornholme JI&N School, Todmorden

Ayrton Widdup	39
Katherine Hearne	39
Alice Butler	40
Lydia Makin	40
Carly Thorp	41
Ola Annie Demkowicz	41
Cyle Chopping	42
Katie Fish	42
William S Butler	42
Ellen Setterfield	43
Luke Simmonds	43
April Walker	44
Oliver Baxter Tannock	44
Jenny Sharphouse	44
Joss Pemsel	45
Steven Whatmough	45
Graham Reid	46
Jamie-Lee Crampton	46

Darnhall Primary School, Winsford

Lois Walsh	47
Jennifer King	47
Cara Turnbull	48
Kelly Curzon	48
Demi Burns	49
Carl Margett	49
Rebecca Lambert & Daniel White	50
Laura Harding	50
Louis Elton & Jack Lloyd	50
Rhiannon Birch & Rebecca Edwards	51
Charlotte Kelsall	51
Alexandra Wheildon	51
Tracy Marriott	52
Peter Long	52

Flowery Field CP School, Hyde

Rebecca Hackett	52
John Taylor	53

Tanmona Ahmed	92
Heidi Forster	92
Cameron Barker	92
Billie-Jo Holden	93
Janine Westwell	93
Joel Alston	94
Mathew Oddie	94
Benjamin Baron	95
Lindsey Barton	96
Dominick Jeal	96

Neston Primary School, Neston

James Archer	97
Roberto Whitley	97
William Flaherty	98
Martin Hannam	98
Stephen Daley	99
Daniel Stone	99
Ryan Butterworth	100
Steven Barnes-Smith	100
Daniel Barraclough	101
Amy Milton	102
Dean Meadows	102
Charlotte Morgan	102
Bethni Maylor	103

Ormskirk CE Primary School, Ormskirk

Danielle Reading	103
Aimee Reeves	104
Laura Caunce	105
Natasha McDonnell	106
Christopher Whitehurst	107
Ben Williams	108
Emily Temple	109
Jade Forshaw	110
Thomas Clegg	111
Bethanie Spears	112
Lauren Gaunt	112
Abigail Bentley	113

Chelsey Mawman	190
Amy Slater	190

St Theresa's RC Primary School, Chester

Adam Gough	191
Stacey Thompson	192
Emily Boyne	193
Shaun Arathoon	194
Nicholas Foster	194
Jessica Withington	195
James Graham	196
Danielle Clutton	197

Statham CP School, Lymm

Ruth Kirk	197
Rebecca Cuffe	198
Peter Booth	198
Kate Kirkwood	199
Rachel Jones	199
Victoria Copley	200
Joseph Broadsmith	200
Josh Boyle	201
Jamie Johnson	201
Hannah Blackwell	202
Sophie Blackwell	202
Joseph Artine	203
Nicola Richards	203
Kieran Crow	203
Katy Burgess	204
Sam Brennan	204
Ryan Green	204
Sarah Hargreaves	205
Paul Hackett	205

Styal Primary School, Wilmslow

Kameel Somani	206
George Massey	207
Heather Talbot	208
Sam Dixon	209

The Poems

CITY SCENE

A   ccountants adding in a busy office block,
B   uyers bustling in the supermarket shop,
C   elebrities calling for a massive crowd of fans,
D   udes dawdling, kicking little cans,
E   ntertainers entertain everything around,
F   actories fire up making a dreadful sound,
G   uys gamble losing all their money,
H   otels' high tops are very sunny
I   ndustries instantly making anything you want,
J   ournalists jot down trying to decide the font,
K   ids kick anything they see,
L   orries load at the side of the quay,
M   otorcycles manoeuvre slowly through the cars,
N   ewsagents' neighbours are shops and bars,
O   ffices opening nine till six,
P   eople playing music and doing tricks,
Q   uangos quarrel with the potential suer,
R   ats running through the sewers,
S   hoppers shopping picking up some wine,
T   rains travelling on the line,
U   mbrellas up for shelter they search,
V   icars verbalising in the church,
W   ardens waiting for time to elapse,
X   enodocheionologists xerox street maps,
Y   ardmen yawn at the end of the day,
Z   ephyrs zigzagged every way.

Adam Bridge (11)

GHOSTS

I saw some *ghosts* upon the stairs,
They were children, walking up in pairs.
It was really very strange, you know,
Because I was standing in a *bungalow*.

Joshua Cox (7)

PUPPY

On Christmas Day
Under the tree
A wriggling box
Presented to me!

When I opened it
Guess what I saw?
An adorable puppy
Sitting up on the floor.

Now this little cute puppy
(Who's black and white)
He may look sweet
But this is really what he's like.

He chews on your slippers
Brings mud on the floor
And when a visitor comes
He barks at the door!

Calm down dear ladies
Oh and gentlemen too
If you think this is terrible
Then here's what to do:

So on Christmas Day
Under the tree
If there's a wriggling box
Run quickly to me!

Millie Green (10)

THE HORSE

There once was a horse
Who ran in a course
He wasn't very fast
So he came in last.

He tried to jump
And landed with a bump
He started to dance
And off flew his pants!

Megan Humphrey (10)
Alderley Edge Community Primary School, Alderley Edge

LITTLE DEVILS

One little devil
Ran up the hill
He said to his doctor,
'What shall I do?'

Two little devils
Ran up the hill
They ate a pill
Then started to kill.

Three little devils
Ran down the hill
Jumped up and down
Then had a chill pill.

Four little devils
Went on a course
One wasn't very fast
So he came in last.

Five little devils
Went on a train
Then they fell off
And started to scoff.

Hannah Aymes (9)
Alderley Edge Community Primary School, Alderley Edge

TIME

Time -
The ever spinning wheel
Drinks no water
Eats no meal
Will not stutter
Never stops
Walks through walls
Heeds not locks
Collects our thanks
Takes our curses
Empties our pockets
Fills our purses
Brings us death
Gives us new life
Gives us happiness
Causes us strife
Has no enemy
Has no friend
Brought to the beginning
Brings the end.

Oliver Hope (10)
Alderley Edge Community Primary School, Alderley Edge

A MAN FROM PERU!

There was an old man from Peru
Who had a great big flu
He went to bed
And he turned himself red
And when he woke he was blue!

Hannah Greensides (9)
Alderley Edge Community Primary School, Alderley Edge

WHAT FOOTBALLERS ARE!

Goal-scorers
Nail-biters
Nose-pickers
Mouth-spitters
Bum-scratchers
Ball-snatchers
Penalty-takers
Money-makers
Crowd-pleasers
Fashion-leaders
Male-models
Mollycoddled
Ball-dribblers
Trophy-winners

That's what footballers are.

Natasha Skiadopoulos (10)
Alderley Edge Community Primary School, Alderley Edge

THE ROOM

In the dark and dusty room there hung a spider's web
And . . . and . . . on the haunted rough surface of the floor
Lay scattering skeletons' bones
From the ceiling shadows of faces appeared
Like a shriek of lightning
Look up at the gloomy lighting wires hanging
Like howling creatures snorting
I was petrified
Out of a rusty, battered window I saw a cemetery
And the gravestones stared back at me.

Sophia Kokkinis (10)
Alderley Edge Community Primary School, Alderley Edge

HUGH'S FRIENDS

There was a big kid called Hugh
Who lived in a little green shoe

Who knew a boy called Ben
Who lived in a small musty den

Who knew a man called Leigh
Who lived on a mushy green pea

Who knew a girl called Carol
Who lived in a wet round barrel

Who knew an old man called Fred
Who lived in a dark brown shed

Who knew a sweet little grandma
Who lived in a flash new car

And they all lived happily ever after.

Hugh Kirk (9)
Alderley Edge Community Primary School, Alderley Edge

HELP!

Hullabaloo! Hullabaloo!
What shall we do? What shall I do?
Everyone's screaming here and there
Even the people in their underwear
Lots of noise - lots of screams
What is it? What is it?
There's no ice cream!
What shall I do? What shall I say?
I'm afraid my life will end this day!

Jennifer Robbins (9)
Alderley Edge Community Primary School, Alderley Edge

THE SEARCH FOR THE KUM-KUM BIRD

Three men went in search of the kum-kum bird
With nets and other things
They thought they'd be able to catch the bird
But no, they probably wouldn't.

For the kum-kum bird is clever
The cleverest flying beast
Before they even knew it
The men were swept from their feet.

And so they came back
All bruised and battered
So they had once again been beaten
By the clever kum-kum bird.

The men then learnt their lesson
And never once again
Went hunting in the wilderness
Or saw the kum-kum bird.

Jack Tinner (9)
Alderley Edge Community Primary School, Alderley Edge

THE TREASURE HUNT

We're going on a treasure hunt
We're going across the sea
Until we find the treasure chest.

So we're going to an island
And digging till we find
The big lot of treasure and it will be all mine!

Arjun Sreekumar (10)
Alderley Edge Community Primary School, Alderley Edge

BOOKS ARE LIKE RUNNING

I am running the race
Just keep the pace
There is nothing worse than coming first
That's just the worse
Don't make me run
It isn't fun
It is boring
Just like snoring
It's just like books
It really sucks
Some books are sad
But I am glad
They make me mad.

Ben Jones (9)
Alderley Edge Community Primary School, Alderley Edge

SKALLOGY

Down in the pits of Doom
Where people fall in and go boom!
Up comes the Skallogy
To have a cup of tea
Oh what a glorious day it is
But there's nobody here to kiss
So he climbed out of the pit
Got on his kit
And went for a great big hike
He went away for a year and a day
And couldn't find a place to stay
Until he found somewhere
And luckily it was fair.

Joe Morrison (9)
Alderley Edge Community Primary School, Alderley Edge

TIM AND THE DIVE

There was a young kid called Tim
Who loved to go for a swim
On one dive he went insane
And no one saw him again.

On one dark night
When the moon was big and bright
Tim emerged from the pool
And went to invade the school.

On the way in
He fell into a bin
The garbage man did chuck
The bin into the truck.

The blade did chop
Tim into a drop
Oh the terrible pain
And no one saw Tim again.

George Troup (9)
Alderley Edge Community Primary School, Alderley Edge

DOG

A high jumper
A fast runner
A slimy nose
And fluffy toes
A meat eater
A sloppy tongue
A tail that's long

A catalogue to make me a dog.

Laura Hough (11)
All Saints CE Primary School, Marple

OLD TREES

Different coloured leaves
Swaying in the breeze
So strong
Standing there so long
As twisty as a snake
As long as a lake
Crunchy leaves on the ground
Children all around
Rough bark
Invisible in the dark
Roots in the soil
See them coil
Trees bare
Trees everywhere
Everlasting
Branches tapping on my window
Calling me to come out
But I won't
I will not.

Jamie Clarke (9)
All Saints CE Primary School, Marple

THE TERROR DOWN YOUR SPINE SOUND

When I go to bed and the light is out
I hear a small sound in the dark night
It sounds like a growl but it starts off low
And then it starts to *grow*
It is annoying, it goes down my spine into my ear
But when I wake up it's not even there.

Joseph Grimsley (9)
All Saints CE Primary School, Marple

TALKING AT NIGHT

I heard a noise that you hear at night
It is very annoying and loud
You just can't stop it
You just can't help it
You can't do anything at all

I heard a noise that you hear at night
It is noisy and loud
You just can't stop it
You just can't help it
You can't do anything at all

I heard talking in the night
It makes it hard to sleep
You just can't stop it
You just can't help it
You can't do anything at all.

Hannah Moore (9)
All Saints CE Primary School, Marple

HEDGEHOG

An insect-eater
A leaf-lover
A night-comer
A day-sleeper
A ball-roller
A needle-thrower
A garden-seeker
A hibernator.

A catalogue to make a hedgehog.

Fay Corrigan (10)
All Saints CE Primary School, Marple

NAILS ON A CHALKBOARD

Every time I walk into class
I get a tingling in my back
All I hear is nails on a chalkboard.

I come in from lunch and sit down
Another feeling in my back
Nails on a chalkboard.

I sink down under my chair
Feel like punching something
'Specially nails on a chalkboard.

If I could ban a noise
It would be . . .
Nails on a chalkboard!

Kit Thomas (9)
All Saints CE Primary School, Marple

A MEAT EATER

A meat-eater
A fish-beater

A scaly-thing
A vicious-thing

A fin-viper
A human-ripper

A sea-monster
A bone-crusher

A catalogue to make me a shark.

Darius Babrahani (11)
All Saints CE Primary School, Marple

GUESS WHAT?

It needs a hand or two
When it goes off
I don't know what to do
It's like a bell
Then it goes tick-tock
Yes, that's right, it's an alarm clock!

It is my worst noise
It opens wide
It creaks at night
People open and close them
It makes kids dream wildly
It's got a handle
So guess what it is?

Dianne Burney (10)
All Saints CE Primary School, Marple

FAIRY

Gentle creatures
With glowing features

Magical beings
Strange seeings

Fluttering wings
Colourful things

Different meanings
And sensitive feelings

A catalogue to make me a fairy.

Natalie Jones (11)
All Saints CE Primary School, Marple

SQUEAKING

S   queaking is very, very annoying
Q uietly go up the squeaky stairs
U tterly revolting *squeaking*
E verlasting noise which should be banned
A n irritating noise which is very loud
K icking about and scaring my nan
I   n the noisy, squeaking house
N ear the toilet, near the bath
G *o away you squeaking mouse!*

Joseph Lynch (9)
All Saints CE Primary School, Marple

HAMSTER

Wheel-winder
Bar-chewer

Treat-nibbler
Night-squeaker

Bed-mover
Cage-scratcher.

Carly Downs (10)
All Saints CE Primary School, Marple

BATHROOM MONSTER

There's a creaking on the landing at night
The bathroom monster's here
And it's giving me a fright!

It moves into the bathroom
And it stays there most o' the night.

Then a creaking door slams shut
This really is giving me a fright
Next a noisy gurgle does arise.

The daylight rises
And the bathroom monster flies.

Dan Blackburn (10)
All Saints CE Primary School, Marple

DEATH

Life-shatterer
Fear-bringer

Living-haunterer
Life-lingerer

Unknown-being

A catalogue to make death.

Joshua Williams (10)
All Saints CE Primary School, Marple

SNORING

S   noring! Snoring!
N   o one snore!
O   h snoring
R   un away snoring
I   rritating snoring
N   o it can't be
G   o away snoring.

Sam Watson (9)
All Saints CE Primary School, Marple

A TREE'S MEMORY

The rustle of leaves as the wind blows her frosty breeze
The still trees in their swaying ease
A home for animals and other plants too
The runny sap like soppy goo
The tragic thunder as a dead tree falls
The break of snow like frozen shawls
The leaves it provides with which you may play
Until it comes to its very last day
You cannot name all the trees
That are always being attracted by bumblebees
The whistle of the summer breeze
As it reaches high degrees
Reaching enormously high
Almost touching the cloudy sky
The giant oak that is huge and vast
Only sees the black and white past.

Sam Walters (9)
All Saints CE Primary School, Marple

HAMSTER

A fast runner
A good climber
A sharp biter
A human lover
A noise maker
A tiny tongue
Small and long

A catalogue to make a hamster.

Steven Boond
All Saints CE Primary School, Marple

EARTH

A huge ball
A creator of all

A tree maker
An earthquake shaker

A rain maker
A sea waver

A green jungle
An avalanche fumble

Mountains high that nearly touch the sky

A catalogue to make me the Earth.

Alastair Jones & Zach Mackay (11)
All Saints CE Primary School, Marple

RAT

A black-eyer
A sharp-teether
A food-eater
A hairy-monster
A pointy-facer
A short-legger
A fast-walker
A long-tailer

A catalogue to make me a rat.

Victoria Edwardson (10)
All Saints CE Primary School, Marple

AN ANNOYING SOUND ALPHABET POEM

A   rguments
B   anging on the stairs
C   halk scratching on the blackboard
D   ogs barking
E   lephants trumpeting
F   eet scampering
G   angs of people shouting
H   amsters nibbling bars
I   nstruments playing at night
J   umping on the floor above you
K   ettle whistling
L   aughing parents early in the morning
M   unching crisps when you're watching TV
N   ursery children screaming
O   pening squeaky doors
P   ractising a flute
Q   uickly then loudly running up the stairs
R   ustling of leaves
S   ausages sizzling in a pan
T   rain dashing on the railway
U   nwanted singing
V   enom spitting
W   indow smashing
X   ylophones playing
Y   appy puppies
Z   ipping coats.

Rachael Donlon (9)
All Saints CE Primary School, Marple

THROUGH A TREE'S EYES

The long hard winter has begun to yield,
As I stand alone in my wide open field;
Spring is here and I am starting to grow,
My long thick arms stretch out oh so slow;
And my leaves come to life as I bear my fruit;
Searching for water with my long twisted roots.

The warm summer sun shines down on me,
So at last, long last, I feel like a tree;
My arms are full of life as the birds sing their song,
The squirrels scamper up and down all day long;
Butterflies emerge from their cocoons in the warm daylight
And the wise old owls hoot-hoot all through the night.

The warm weather ends as autumn creeps in,
My long pointed arms are now wearing thin;
My autumn leaves turn red, gold and brown,
As they curl and shrivel before falling down;
The wind blows through my arms with a howling sound,
Rustling the leaves and scattering them all around.

As winter comes and my arms grow tired and old,
I shiver and tremble as I feel the cold;
With the rain and the frost and blankets of snow,
I can't wait for the cold dark winter go to;
As Christmas comes I see people full of glee
And so ends the year in the life of this tree.

Dean Dowling (9)
All Saints CE Primary School, Marple

THE FOUR SEASONS OF A TREE

A ladder to nothingness, towards the sky
Peeling bark dropping with a sigh.

Leaves somersaulting here and there
I see from the window as I stare.

Brown, green, red and yellow
Falling in the twang of a cello.

The branches of an old oak tree
Ushering you closer, welcomingly.

In the same place it always lingers
Forking out like wispy fingers.

As winter very slowly passes
The leaves have settled in soggy masses.

But soon spring comes, with it new buds
Other trees grow creating woods.

The trees grow leaves in the click of a finger
Birds make nests whistling like a singer.

To everyone's delight summer comes
The birds fly off to become dads and mums.

But as before as if in a circle
Autumn comes and now the leaves *hurtle!*

James Collett (10)
All Saints CE Primary School, Marple

BABY

Pram-snuggler
Mum-cuddler
Loud-screamer
Heavy-dreamer

Fast-crawler
Grows-taller
Milk-drinker
Nappy-stinker

Dummy-sucker
Blanket-lover

A catalogue to make me a baby.

Laura Carter (10)
All Saints CE Primary School, Marple

CAT

Milk-drinker
Quick-thinker
Face-scratcher
Mouse-catcher
Sharp-claws
Vicious-jaws
Bad-swimmer
Growing-thinner.

Ben Kadler (10)
All Saints CE Primary School, Marple

THE WORST NOISES EVER

It's my worst noise ever
I have lots of them
You want to hear them?
Here we go

A   larm clocks
B   ees buzzing
C   halk scraping down the blackboard
D   ucks quacking
E   agles in the sky
F   rogs jumping
G   uns banging
H   orses neighing
I   rons smoking
J   unk falling
K   ids screaming
L   awn mowers
M   oney clanging
N   oises everywhere
O   lympic crowds
P   eople speaking
Q   ueen screaming
R   ain pouring on the roof
S   nakes sliding around the grass
T   he wildlife
U   mbrellas flapping
V   ans going over bumps
W   hite board pens squeaking
X   mas paper being torn apart
Y   oung babies crying
Z   oo animals everywhere.

Kealey Wilson (10)
All Saints CE Primary School, Marple

WHEN I GROW UP

When I grow up
I would like to be
A screaming woman
With a baby.

When I grow up
I would like to be
The master
At geography.

When I grow up
I would like to be
The owner of
A cemetery.

When I grow up
I would like to be
The coldest can
Of Pepsi.

When I grow up
I would like to be
The president
Of all eternity.

When I grow up
I would like to be
A star fighter
In a galaxy.

Matthew Birt (8)
Christ Church CE Primary School, Ellesmere Port

WHEN I GROW UP

When I grow up
I would like to be
a professional footballer
on national TV.

When I grow up
I would like to be
a mad person
who lives in the galaxy.

When I grow up
I would like to be
a person
who makes history.

When I grow up
I would like to be
a rich and famous person
but not on TV.

When I grow up
I would like to be
not me
but a royal majesty.

Garry Bebbington (8)
Christ Church CE Primary School, Ellesmere Port

I SPEAK, I SAY

Dogs growl, bats click
Sheep baa, kittens miaow
Dinosaurs roar, dolphins eek
Elephants trumpet, but I speak!

Giraffes chomp, dodos flap
Rhinoceros groan, mice squeak
Snakes hiss, horses neigh
Chickens cluck, but I say!

Robert Bellis (8)
Christ Church CE Primary School, Ellesmere Port

WHEN I GROW UP

When I grow up
I would like to be
a master
of capacity.

When I grow up
I would like to be
a soldier awarded
for bravery.

When I grow up
I would like to be
a rich man
for all eternity.

When I grow up
I would like to be
a spy for our
Royal Majesty.

When I grow up
I would like to be
me!

Graeme Roberts (8)
Christ Church CE Primary School, Ellesmere Port

Cows

C ows are fat and round
O h, cows are strong
W hy are cows so big?
S o why can't they be thin like us?

C ows make milk, why?
O h, how yummy it tastes!
W hy do they do this for us?
S o I appreciate that.

C ows make butter, why?
O h, how good it tastes on bread!
W hy, oh why does this happen!
S o let's give three big cheers to the cows!

C ows are a little annoying
O h what do they make that infernal mooing sound?
W hy and how do they make that sound?
S o we can't blame them because they were born this way.

Paul Young (9)
Christ Church CE Primary School, Ellesmere Port

When I Grow Up

When I grow up I would like to be
A popaholic who only drinks Pepsi

When I grow up I would like to be
The best presenter on TV

When I grow up I would like to be
A mermaid in the deep blue sea.

When I grow up I would like to be
An explorer in the zoology.

When I grow up I would like to be
An explorer in the galaxy.

Katie Pitchford (8)
Christ Church CE Primary School, Ellesmere Port

WHEN I GROW UP

When I grow up
I would like to be
the best footballer
for Man City.

When I grow up
I would like to be
a man who drinks
a load of Pepsi.

When I grow up
I would like to be
the king of all
society.

When I grow up
I would like to be
an old man
who's 150.

When I grow up
I would like to be
me!

Alex Goodwin (8)
Christ Church CE Primary School, Ellesmere Port

YELLOW

What is yellow?
It is all the brightness of the world
It is the sun
How does it feel?
It is better and it is happiness
Yellow
It sounds like spring
What is yellow?
It is life.

Calum Mclean (9)
Christ Church CE Primary School, Ellesmere Port

BLUE

Blue
It is the ocean driving forwards
It is the rich colour of the sky
It is the colour of coldness, frosty and icy
Blue
It is the scent of flowers
The colour of sadness
It is small
It is the colour of water
Blue.

Mark Ashbrook (9)
Christ Church CE Primary School, Ellesmere Port

WHEN I GROW UP

When I grow up
I would like to be
a famous person
who lives on the TV.

When I grow up
I would like to be
the best
at robbing jewellery.

Willis Pritchard (8)
Christ Church CE Primary School, Ellesmere Port

WHEN I GROW UP

When I grow up
I would like to be
a popaholic
that drinks Pepsi.

When I grow up
I would like to be
the best soldier
in the navy.

When I grow up
I would like to be
a beautiful mermaid
in the deep blue sea.

When I grow up
I would like to be
an old lady
that's sixty.

When I grow up
I would like to be
me!

Lauren Killcross (8)
Christ Church CE Primary School, Ellesmere Port

WHEN I GROW UP

When I grow up
I would like to be
a hot cup of tea.

When I grow up
I would like to be
famous on TV.

When I grow up
I would like to be
a mermaid in the deep blue sea.

When I grow up
I would like to be
in a movie on TV.

When I grow up
I would like to be
a soldier in the army.

Jodie Breen (9)
Christ Church CE Primary School, Ellesmere Port

WHITE

White
It is the sky above
It is all the brightness of the sky
It is soft and relaxing.

White
It is the sound of lightness everywhere
The sound of the softest bear ever
It is the colour of white
It is the best white!

Charlie Roberts (9)
Christ Church CE Primary School, Ellesmere Port

A COLOUR

Yellow
It is the colour of the sun
It is all the riches in the world
Yellow
It is the colour of summer
And the desert
Yellow
It is the colour of bananas
And happiness
Yellow
It is the colour of cars, books and posters
Yellow
It is the colour of my pen.

Ryan Kendal (9)
Christ Church CE Primary School, Ellesmere Port

SUMMER

Summer
It is a bright orange
It is a joyful season
It is boiling hot.
Summer
It is the sound of children playing
The sound of birds tweeting
It is the colour gold
It is life
Summer.

Lauren Kavanagh (9)
Christ Church CE Primary School, Ellesmere Port

MY POEM

One wet whale went wiggling west
Two terrible terrapins tested tinsel
Three thin thrushes thanked the thieves
Four frightened foxes fiddled with food
Five fish fingers fired thimbles
Six sick seagulls smelt of smelly socks
Seven slithering snakes smelt of sausages
Eight ageing apes lived on apricots
Nine naughty newts spoke to knickers
Ten teasing turtles tickled tigers.

Jasmine Green (7)
Christ Church CE Primary School, Ellesmere Port

ALLITERATION POEM

One wicked witch went wandering into the wet town
Two terrible turtles took the TV
Three talking TVs took the thrushes
Four funny frogs fell by a funny fox
Five foolish foxes fell flat on their faces
Six smelly socks slithered slowly
Seven stupid switches smell bad
Eight elephants eat everything
Nine nannies knitting nicely
Ten terrapins talking terribly.

Eric Ankers (7)
Christ Church CE Primary School, Ellesmere Port

ANIMAL ALLITERATION

One wet whale went west to wash
Two terrible terrapins took treasure to Tinseltown
Three thin thrushes threw things
Four frightened foxes found four feathers
Five fish fingers free fall forever
Six sick seagulls save Sam
Seven slithering snakes slithered south
Eight ageing apes are annoying
Nine naughty newts went north
Ten teasing turtles took treasure.

Jordan Conlong (7)
Christ Church CE Primary School, Ellesmere Port

MY POEM

One wet whale went wiggling wildly
Two terrible terrapins' tails took tape from Tangoland
Three thin thrushes threaded through the thorns
Four frightened foxes fiddled with fudge
Five fish fingers fought for food
Six sick seagulls smelt smelly
Seven slithering snakes smelt of smelly socks
Eight ageing apes ached for apples
Nine naughty newts knelled up
Ten teasing turtles took treasure from Tropical Island.

Chelsea Butler (8)
Christ Church CE Primary School, Ellesmere Port

My Alliteration Poem

One white willow tree waving in the wind
Two terrible turtles took some treasure
Three thrashing thrushes took the toothpaste
Four foul frogs filled some fish with fillings
Five funny fish fell over
Six silly slimeballs slithered away
Seven stupid swimmers swimming slowly
Eight old elephants ate every egg
Nine knitting nannies knitting nicely
Ten teasing terrapins took Thomas' telly.

Calum Doolan (8)
Christ Church CE Primary School, Ellesmere Port

Animal Alliterations

One wet whale went wandering west
Two terrible terrapins tried to eat a train
Three thoughtful thrushes threw a thin thunderstorm
Four frightened foxes found food
Five fish fingers fiddled through fire
Six sick seagulls smelt socks
Seven slithering snakes slimed
Eight ageing apes ate apples
Nine naughty newts nicked knickers
Ten teasing turtles told tales.

Thomas Harding (8)
Christ Church CE Primary School, Ellesmere Port

ANIMAL ALLITERATIONS

One wet whale was wiggling west
Two terrible terrapins tried to tip a trolley
Three thin thrushes threw tennis balls on Thursday
Four frightened foxes flew far away
Five fish fingers fought for food
Six sick seagulls swam to shore
Seven slithering snakes slithered to Snakeland
Eight ageing apes ate apples
Nine naughty newts never knew nice newts ate nits
Ten teasing turtles taught a team.

Sean Grisedale (8)
Christ Church CE Primary School, Ellesmere Port

ANIMAL ALLITERATIONS

One wet whale went west
Two terrible terrapins took the TV
Three thin thrushes throw the ball today
Four frightened foxes flew in the air
Five fish fingers sitting on the TV
Six sick seagulls flew around the sea
Seven slithering snakes slithering around
Eight ageing apes eating apples all night
Nine naughty newts nibbling all night
Ten teasing turtles are ten today.

Ben Sutton (7)
Christ Church CE Primary School, Ellesmere Port

ANIMAL ALLITERATIONS

One white whale walked with William
Two terrible terrapins tapped tall trees
Three thin thrushes threw thunder
Four frightened foxes fancy Frankenstein
Five fish fingers frozen fantastically
Six sick seagulls safely sailing
Seven slithering snakes slightly slither
Eight ageing apes ate apple crumble
Nine naughty newts nicked nappies
Ten teasing tigers taught teachers.

Faith Spencer Shone (7)
Christ Church CE Primary School, Ellesmere Port

MY POEM

One white willow tree waved in the wind
Two terrible turtles took the treasure
Three thrashing thrushes took the toothpaste
Four foul frogs found fish
Five funny things fell over
Six silly snakes slithered away
Seven sick swimmers swam away
Eight old elephants ate an egg
Nine knitting nannies knitting nicely
Ten teasing toads took Thomas' toy.

Connor Mckeown (7)
Christ Church CE Primary School, Ellesmere Port

ANIMAL ALLITERATION

One wet whale wiggled to the whip
Two terrible terrapins tangled the tape
Three thin thrushes threaded a table
Four frightened foxes feasted on a fairy
Five fish fingers fiddled frequently
Six sick seagulls in the sky smiled
Seven slithering snakes smelt of soap
Eight ageing apes were afraid
Nine naughty newts nicked nanny
Ten teasing turtles tackled Thomas.

Elinor Jewkes (7)
Christ Church CE Primary School, Ellesmere Port

ANIMAL ALLITERATION

One wet whale went west
Two terrible terrapins took tinsel
Three thin thrushes threw tennis balls
Four frightened foxes found fudge
Five fish fingers found footballs
Six sick seagulls sucked soup
Seven slithering snakes being sick
Eight ageing apes ate apples
Nine naughty newts nibbled nuts
Ten teasing turtles took turns to tango.

Lauren Rees (8)
Christ Church CE Primary School, Ellesmere Port

ANIMAL ALLITERATIONS

One wet whale wiggled west
Two terrible terrapins took treasure to town
Three thin thrushes threw tennis balls
Four frightened foxes fiddled and fidgeted
Five fish fingers found fudge
Six sick seagulls stood still
Seven slithering snakes were sick
Eight ageing apes ate apples
Nine naughty newts took knickers
Ten teasing turtles took tape.

Elizabeth Lambert (7)
Christ Church CE Primary School, Ellesmere Port

ANIMAL ALLITERATION

One wet whale walked to the waterfall
Two terrible terrapins told tall tales
Three thin thrushes flew to the theatre
Four frightened foxes found fifty fleas
Five fish fingers found the forest
Six sick seagulls stuffed with sausages
Seven slithering snakes sang a song
Eight ageing ape made alligator pie
Nine naughty newts never knew Neal
Ten terrible terrapins told the time.

Joe McLeod (8)
Christ Church CE Primary School, Ellesmere Port

ZORDINEX

Zordinex has -
hair as soft as tissue,
a head as strong as steel,
eyes like lasers.
Teeth as sharp as knives,
neck as thick as a tree trunk,
arms as thin as a stick.
Fingers as pointed as a pyramid,
belly as fat as an elephant,
legs as thin as a ruler.
Feet as round as a football,
toes as small as a pin.

Ayrton Widdup (8)
Cornholme JI&N School, Todmorden

CHRISTMAS

C   hristmas is a lovely day,
H   ow you smile and play,
R   un up and down the hall,
I   have fun at Christmas,
S   ome people dance around the Christmas tree,
T   op of the sky is Santa and his sleigh,
M   um making a Christmas cake,
A   s Santa's sleigh swoops past the window,
S   o settle down into bed and sleep till tomorrow.

Katherine Hearne (8)
Cornholme JI&N School, Todmorden

FRED THE JUMPING CATERPILLAR

Fed has -

A face as round as a plate
Eyes as brown as a bear
Nostrils like sunflowers
Lips as red as Mars
A chin like a ball
A body as long as two metres
Legs as strong as a wrestler
Toes like an orange
A tummy as fit as a gym teacher
Smells like a pigsty
Sound like a mouse squeaking
Jumps like a rabbit.

Alice Butler (8)
Cornholme JI&N School, Todmorden

STARLIGHT

Starlight has -
hair like a rabbit,
eyebrows like a horse's tail,
eyes as round as marbles,
a nose as pointed as a triangle,
a mouth as round as a top on a semicircle,
a neck as small as a rabbit's foot,
arms as long as a giraffe's neck,
feet smaller than a mouse,
legs as strong as a bull.

Lydia Makin (8)
Cornholme JI&N School, Todmorden

BLUE

Blue is the sea
Sparkling in the sun.
Blue is the sky,
I don't know why.
Blue is distress,
A lot of sadness.
Blue is the colour of bluebells,
Stood straight and proud.
Blue is people crying,
Really loud.
The colour of your eyes,
What surprise!
Blue is the colour of your paintings,
Pictures of a whale,
All wrinkled and frail.
Blue, blue, blue, blue, blue.
Blue is the best!

Carly Thorp (9)
Cornholme JI&N School, Todmorden

THANK YOU POEM

Dear Granny,

I've never got such a big pot of earth,
Or a packet of seeds sellotaped at its side,
They shouldn't take too long to grow,
Should they now?
My plant from last time grew,
Then straight away died.

Ola Annie Demkowicz (10)
Cornholme JI&N School, Todmorden

DON'T FORGET YOUR CAPITAL LETTERS AND FULL STOPS

You can forget to do your homework
or forget to clean your snake out.
You can forget to clean the loo
or forget to go to school.
You can forget to fill your water bottle
or forget to clean your tops.
But don't forget your capital letters
and full stops.

Cyle Chopping (9)
Cornholme JI&N School, Todmorden

DON'T FORGET YOUR CAPITAL LETTERS AND FULL STOPS

You can forget to do your homework
or forget to tie your shoes.
You can forget to clean your snake out
or forget to clean your teeth.
You can forget to do your maths work
or forget to wash your tops.
But don't forget your capital letters
and full stops!

Katie Fish (8)
Cornholme JI&N School, Todmorden

DON'T FORGET YOUR CAPITAL LETTERS AND FULL STOPS

You can forget to go to school
or forget to clean your teeth.
You can forget to eat your breakfast
or forget to do your maths.

You can forget to fill your water bottle
or forget to call the cops.
But don't forget your capital letters
and *full stops!*

William S Butler (9)
Cornholme JI&N School, Todmorden

DON'T FORGET YOUR CAPITAL LETTERS AND FULL STOPS

You can forget to do your homework
or forget to brush your shoes.
You can forget to use a ruler
or forget to clean your teeth.
You can forget to clean your snake out
or forget to go to the shops.
But don't forget your capital letters
and full stops!

Ellen Setterfield (8)
Cornholme JI&N School, Todmorden

DON'T FORGET YOUR CAPITAL LETTERS AND FULL STOPS

You can forget to do your homework
or forget to blow your nose.
You can forget to spike your hair up
or forget to clean your shoes.
You can forget to get your presents
or forget to change your socks.
But don't forget your capital letters
and *full stops!*

Luke Simmonds (8)
Cornholme JI&N School, Todmorden

YESTERDAY, TODAY, TOMORROW POEM

Yesterday I lit all the burning fires in the world.
I flew high and low, up and down.
I was a firefly.

Today I am eating all the fish in the sea,
Swimming and swooping.
I am a dolphin.

Tomorrow I will raid the vegetable store,
Run and hop.
I will be a rabbit.

April Walker (9)
Cornholme JI&N School, Todmorden

DEAR UNCLE

Dear Uncle,

Great socks, quite charming I think
It's funny how all the girls start to wink
And how did you know my favourite colour was pink?
They'll also go well with my denim jeans.

Oliver Baxter Tannock (11)
Cornholme JI&N School, Todmorden

THE THING!

8 ruby blazing eyes,
staring, glaring, peering, scaring.
5 blue muddy claws,
scratching, gripping, ripping, slashing.

10 red bloodthirsty fangs,
ripping, biting, chewing, tearing.
230 multicoloured slimy scales,
slivering through the mouldy pond.

Jenny Sharphouse (10)
Cornholme JI&N School, Todmorden

NEMESIS

Nemesis has -
hair as spiky as knives,
a head as strong as rock,
eyes like windows,
a nose like a mountain,
chest as big as a hill,
a waist as hard as iron,
arms as big as the Eiffel Tower,
feet that bang like thunder.

Joss Pemsel (8)
Cornholme JI&N School, Todmorden

DEAR UNCLE

Dear Uncle,

What a jumper
Now I'll know what to wear.
This must definitely be the style
And I'm certain you're right,
That I'll stand out a mile!

Steven Whatmough (11)
Cornholme JI&N School, Todmorden

ZORDLOCK

Zordlock has -
hair as soft as a pillow,
a head as strong as steel,
eyes like a light bulb,
neck as strong as a tree trunk,
nose as big as a mountain,
ears as pointy as a pencil,
shoulders as wide as the Atlantic Ocean,
arms as long as a lamp post,
fingers as pointy as a pyramid,
nails as small as a pin,
legs as slimy as a snake,
toes as fat as a chimney,
toenails as round as a bauble.

Graham Reid (8)
Cornholme JI&N School, Todmorden

THE EXTERMINATOR

The Exterminator has -
eyes like two red ping-pong balls,
ears as big as two shuttles,
a neck that looks like a big metal pole,
shoulders as long as the wall of China,
arms as thin as a pencil lead,
a chest like rock hard armour,
a voice like a robot,
a thigh as strong as a rock,
legs as big as a tree trunk,
feet that look like a skeleton's feet.

Jamie-Lee Crampton (8)
Cornholme JI&N School, Todmorden

NO MAN CAN KILL HIM

The first is the stag, the second is the water,
The third is the fire that falls before the snow.
The spring slithers down the hill,
The wild wind rocks the trees,
The glowing glisten of the fire sends a shiver through the hall,
Frozen to the marrow by the cold snow.

For Beowulf, the might warrior comes, comes to conquer all.

Darkness deepens, weather change
And all will never be the same.
As he creeps he whispers a name,
A name so vile you will never forget

Grendel!

Lois Walsh (11)
Darnhall Primary School, Winsford

PLEEEEEEEEEASE!

Give me a tiger that can take me to Disneyland.
I'll die for a hat that could give me as many wishes as I want.
I want a picture book which can move like a motorbike
And a bed which shows me the future.
I need a racing car which lets me win every race.
Come on, give me a kettle which can make any kind of drink.
I'd like a tree that could bring me the stars
And a box which can give me all of the gold I need.
I'm having a dolphin that can take me to the most beautiful beach ever
And a door which takes me to a different island every week.
Can I have a robot which cleans up after me?

Jennifer King (9)
Darnhall Primary School, Winsford

ON THE FARM, IN THE DARK

On the farm in the dark, I hear the wind blowing
round my house.
On the farm in the dark, I hear the branches of a
tree snap as the wind gets stronger.
On the farm in the dark I stand and listen to the
wind behind me.
On the farm in the dark I hear an owl screech as she
feeds her young.
On the farm in the dark I hear fox cubs cry for their
mother to come.
On the farm in the dark I hear the badgers rustling in
their holes.
On the farm in the dark I hear the rats scurrying in my
horse's fresh hay.
On the farm in the dark I hear the horses stamp as the
wind hits them.

That's what happens when you're on the farm in the dark.

Cara Turnbull (10)
Darnhall Primary School, Winsford

GRENDEL

Bloodsucking fangs,
Hairy, aggressive,
Vicious, angry,
Fast, venomous,
Fearsome, scary,
Green, bumpy,
Scaly skin.
Grendel!

Kelly Curzon (10)
Darnhall Primary School, Winsford

MEDUSA

Teeth as sharp as an axe,
Teeth as long as the journey from Willow Wood.
Teeth like pouncing tigers.
Teeth as black as black cats.
Teeth as mucky as can be.
Eyes like yellow faces
Eyes like they are turning into frogs.
Eyes like silver spoons.
Eyes as hairy as monkeys.
Eyes as black as rain.
Eyes as white as a ghost's mouth.
Hair as blue as can be.
Hair as thick as a train door.
Hair like leaping fish.
Hair as sharp as a whale's fin.
Claws as long as a school field.
Claws as crooked as a house lane.
Tongue like a roller coaster drop.

Demi Burns (11)
Darnhall Primary School, Winsford

WACKY WILDLIFE

Imagine a gorilla who went out with a chinchilla.
Imagine a horse who was in the Royal Airforce.
Imagine a lion who went flyin'.
Imagine a monkey who was so funky.
Imagine a spider who was drinking cider.
Imagine an eel who went out with a seal.
Imagine a croc who was fixing a clock.
Imagine a snake eating a Flake.

Carl Margett (10)
Darnhall Primary School, Winsford

GRENDEL

Grendel, Grendel,
Over the moors,
Into the great hall.

Grendel, Grendel,
Hair like string in knots,
His face covered in green slimy hair,
One eye glowing like the sun.

Grendel!

Rebecca Lambert (10) & Daniel White (9)
Darnhall Primary School, Winsford

WHAT IS BLUE?

What is blue? Streams are blue, floating through.
What is gold? Pennies are gold, kept in a till so old.
What is black? Shadows are black, moving from your back.
What is red? A teddy is red, sitting on your bed.
What is orange? An orange is orange, just an orange.

Laura Harding (10)
Darnhall Primary School, Winsford

GRENDEL

Grendel lurches in the trees,
Going house-to-house, killing anyone he sees,
Creeping up to the stag.

Moaning and groaning, he opened the door,
Killing the warriors he sees,
Running back till the next night.

Louis Elton & Jack Lloyd (10)
Darnhall Primary School, Winsford

BEOWOLF

Scary, worried eyes,
Frightened warrior *run!*
Grendel's arm twisting,
Running from Beowulf.
Poisonous blood spilt in the hall,
Waterwolf crying.

Rhiannon Birch & Rebecca Edwards (11)
Darnhall Primary School, Winsford

CHARLIE'S CRAZY CREATURES

Imagine a lizard who was in love with a wizard,
Imagine a duck that hated muck.
Imagine a frog frantic in the fog.
Imagine a baboon dancing with the moon.
Imagine a monkey whose arms were chunky.
Imagine a dolphin whose dad went out golfing.

Charlotte Kelsall (10)
Darnhall Primary School, Winsford

THE INSECTS

It was so silent I heard an ant nibbling on a crumb.
It was so peaceful I heard an earwig digging for wax.
It was so calm I heard a spider crawling round and round.
It was so still I heard a snail slithering up the bark of a tree.
It was so tranquil that I heard a load of insects
Scurrying, slithering and crawling around and around.

Alexandra Wheildon (10)
Darnhall Primary School, Winsford

SENSES

It was so calm that I heard a tiny raindrop splash on the ground,
It was so still that I felt the morning breeze blow past me,
It was so tranquil that I saw a leaf floating in the nearest pond.
It was so peaceful I smelled a bird open its wings and fly away.
It was so fresh that I could taste the breeze surrounding me.

Tracy Marriott (11)
Darnhall Primary School, Winsford

GRENDEL

Darkness-lover,
Light-hater,
Blood-drinker,
Flesh-eater.

Laughter-hater,
Roar-lover,
Man-ripper,
Neck-snapper.

Man-eater
Life-taker
Who am I?

Peter Long (9)
Darnhall Primary School, Winsford

ARE YOU SCARED OF THE DARK?

Do you feel ever so scared
When the ghost creeps out at night?

Do you feel the slither of the closet snake
As it slides up your leg?

Do you hear the roar of the monster
That hides under your bed?

But most of all, are you scared
Of the huge, dark, quilt?

It silently creeps and slides
Through the bedroom door at night.

You think you're safe
But the darkness will return.

Rebecca Hackett (10)
Flowery Field CP School, Hyde

HURRICANE

I hope he doesn't come again,
That nasty Mister Hurricane.

You see that man, he's not polite,
He sends farm animals into flight,
And every time that man did sneeze,
He bent back metal and huge trees,
He took his claws and scratched the land.

I hope he doesn't come again,
That nasty Mister Hurricane.

He ate our houses and homes,
Disconnected lights and phones,
And when he'd had enough fun,
He left as quickly as he'd come.

I hope he doesn't come again,
That nasty Mister Hurricane.

John Taylor (10)
Flowery Field CP School, Hyde

FEARS OF A MOUSE

Owls fly, foxes run, frogs jump,
I can't escape no matter how I try

I am a mouse, these are my fears
Plus more and I normally end up in tears
They are big and sometimes tall
And because I'm a mouse I am very small.

Owls fly, foxes run, frogs jump,
I can't escape no matter how I try.

You see me as a pest and I guess that's the best thing to call me.
I am slick and I am quick and as dynamic as a flea.

Owls fly, foxes run, frogs jump,
I can't escape no matter how I try.

Last thing to say and I can do it with ease,
Is outdo a mousetrap and get the cheese.

Nathan Johnson (9)
Flowery Field CP School, Hyde

ANATOMY OF LIFE

Burrowing underground,
Anchoring and searching for food.

Torso standing boldly,
Wrinkled, shrivelled shell.

Gradually expanding limbs,
Floating canopy, scattering evenly.

Delicate fingers, stretching evenly,
Gripping the baby buds cautiously.

Energy waiting to explode,
Blossoms springing into life.

Becky Hackett (10), Nathan Johnson & Jessica Davis (9)
& Mary Openshaw (8)
Flowery Field CP School, Hyde

ROLLER COASTER

I'm going so fast, I feel all funny
I feel something hurting, inside my tummy.

I want it to stop
Or I'll come off, like a mop.
I'll look like a scarecrow
My hair like an Aero.

I fly out of my seat as I go
Over a bump!
It's like riding on a big
Camel's hump!

It's slowing down, well, phew I'm glad,
But now, I am very, very sad.

I spent a lot of money on that
Massive ride.
When all I did was cry
And cry.

Sarah Chapman (11)
Hurst Knoll CE Primary School, Ashton-under-Lyne

THE WAR

The world is filled with sadness
The people cry and pray
The people cry for peace and joy
But that won't come today

The bombs are loud and noisy
I hate the bangs they make
And when they come to take our lives
The peace of the country dies
The people shiver and shake
With all the bangs they make

I wish it would end and we could all be friends
They always ruin our lives
I hate it when they do

Adolf Hitler was the German leader
And a terrible bad reader
Britain was a good land
But now it's filled with sand

At the start of the war
I had to do some chores
To invade Britain, Hitler knew how
Then Germany and Britain had a big row.

Samantha Bardsley (9)
Hurst Knoll CE Primary School, Ashton-under-Lyne

EVACUEE

I was at home, very happy
When World War II broke out, very snappy.
My brother and I were whispering to each other
About my mum going to a factory
But my dad was hoping for victory.

My brother and I were talking to each other
When we left home.
We were on the train
When we saw a massive frame
Carrying a 2,000 pound bomb.

Mick Clegg (10)
Hurst Knoll CE Primary School, Ashton-under-Lyne

SLEEPLESS NIGHT

Street lights flash
Cars pass,
Silence can't be heard.
A shadow appears
Something catches my ears,
Oh, it's just a bird!

Noise is too loud
My heart does pound,
My head is spinning fast
I feel my eyes well up with tears.
How much can I take?
I've too many fears.

I shoot up in bed
Is everyone dead?
My pillow is wet
I'm covered in sweat.
How much can I take?

I walk over to the window,
Slowly, carefully.
To my surprise and to my shock,
All I could see was the scene
From my nightmare.

Teona Racheal Horrocks (11)
Hurst Knoll CE Primary School, Ashton-under-Lyne

THE LONELY WAR

I stand here looking out at all of my friends
I cry because my family and friends are lying there dying,
minute after minute.
I stand there alone in the trench,
water up to my knees.
Rats who nibble on my pants, go away
and return with more.

I stand shivering, the only surviving child,
I have nowhere to go except for the cold
and lonely trench.
No houses left, just standing in the trench
I cry for hours and hours, with no one to calm me down.

All I have to keep me warm is a small blanket,
it's not enough to keep me warm.
All I really want to do is to go home,
I know I shouldn't have been here in the first place.

Kirstie Hanlon (11)
Hurst Knoll CE Primary School, Ashton-under-Lyne

BLACKOUT

The blackout is a horrible thing,
It is as dark as a black jaguar.
The blackout is horrible.

You do not want
to be in the
blackout!

Brandon Bradbury (9)
Hurst Knoll CE Primary School, Ashton-under-Lyne

ROCKET TRIP

I do feel nervous
My blood pressure is going high
Getting in my rocket
To go way up in the sky.

Rumbling here
Rumbling there
I feel like I'm
Rumbling everywhere.

I'm getting something from the sensor
It's showing planet Mars
To move around quickly
I'll get in my space car.

It's pretty dark out here
And Mars is pretty red
Once I have got home again
I'll get back into bed.

Axel J Wolfe (10)
Hurst Knoll CE Primary School, Ashton-under-Lyne

I NEED YOU

Me for you and you for me,
I need you and you need me.
You are fab, you are sweet,
You are nice and tidy and you are neat.
I like you because you are my love.

Joshua Turner (10)
Hurst Knoll CE Primary School, Ashton-under-Lyne

BOMBING

The cries of the bombing
Is leaving me sobbing
For my mum and dad.
I wish I was at home
In my very safe dome
As I'm only a six-year-old lad.

I'm singing a rhyme
While I'm playing with the chime.
But the bombing is still going on
And the Jerries are tired
Neil is fired -
All of the sun has gone.

Even though war's done
We know that we've won.
I'm with my mum and dad
We are safely home and glad.

Adam Smith (9)
Hurst Knoll CE Primary School, Ashton-under-Lyne

ALL ALONE

Time stands still
I wait for you.
You're not there
I feel a little chill.

I hear a creak
I suddenly feel weak
And I don't know what to do,
As I still stand here and wait for you.

There is a knock on the door,
So I jump to the floor.
I open it and to my surprise,
I see you stood outside.
I am not alone any more
Since you knocked on my door.

Toni Frattaroli (10)
Hurst Knoll CE Primary School, Ashton-under-Lyne

MUM

You're so cool
You're so good,
You're so nice
You're so fab.
You're so thin
You're so great,
You're so sweet,
You're the best -
You're my mum.

Kane Stimpson (10)
Hurst Knoll CE Primary School, Ashton-under-Lyne

GAS

Gas, gas, wherever you go, gas, gas I say, 'No!'
Gas, gas, my dad says gas has to stay.
I might as well go astray,
Gas, gas, it's not fair why didn't they send some air.
Gas, gas, gas, gas, gas all the time and I like rhyme.
Not gas!

Robert Gorton (10)
Hurst Knoll CE Primary School, Ashton-under-Lyne

EVACUEE

I was scared of the evacuee,
My parents were sailing on the sea.
I thought they drowned of fright.

In the dark and spooky night,
I heard that they didn't drown.
I was then jumping like a clown
My parents then came home.

When I thought I'd broken my bone,
I was hearing all the bombs drop - loud.
Then trying to make a loud sound,
I then went to have my tea,
Then my mum came for me.

Hayley Hardy (9)
Hurst Knoll CE Primary School, Ashton-under-Lyne

WHEN I'M FEELING

When I'm feeling lonely
I'm only and only lonely.
I have nothing to do
Or nowhere to go.

When I'm feeling sad
I'm only and only sad.
I cry and cry
Then sigh.

But when I'm feeling happy,
I'm very, very happy.
I laugh and laugh
And always smile.

Meera Mistry (10)
Hurst Knoll CE Primary School, Ashton-under-Lyne

ME, YOU AND THE WAR

When I'm lying in my comfy bed,
Thoughts are running through my restless head
And I know there are soldiers and people dead
In that terrible war.
My dad might be lying on the muddy floor
Whilst Mum and me are becoming poor
And when I am asleep
I dream that Mum and I weep
About my dad,
Even though he's not a lad,
Whilst we think of our loved ones,
People are dropping dreadful bombs.
If you hear Hitler's name
Remember he's to blame.

Briony Bradbury (10)
Hurst Knoll CE Primary School, Ashton-under-Lyne

FOR MY GIRLFRIEND (NOT)

You're so fab
You're so great
You're so nice
You're so good
You're my hobby
You're my dream
You love me
I love you
You're my lovely football
You're my lovely football kit
You're my lovely Lunar Predators!

Anthony Baron-Shaw (11)
Hurst Knoll CE Primary School, Ashton-under-Lyne

ALL ALONE

I am sitting here in my chair,
Staring out at the countryside,
Feeling bored as if I'd died.

All alone, no one cares,
The sun is joining my
Feeling dead.
Darkness draws in
The sun goes to bed.
Leaving me all alone, no one cares,
I hear a noise
What is that?
I'm scared, I'm all alone -
Oh, it's a bird, flying home.

Danielle Shauney Andrew (10)
Hurst Knoll CE Primary School, Ashton-under-Lyne

WAR

The peace before,
We really wanted more
The silence that had ruled
Had come to a sad end.

Blasting bombs, calling captains.
It's a great shame
And Hitler is to blame.

Jade Arnell (10)
Hurst Knoll CE Primary School, Ashton-under-Lyne

INSIDE MY TUMMY

The wind blew strong
And carried me along,
I felt all funny inside
My tummy.
I flew past my class,
Way too fast.
My class said
I'm funny, but
I think I'm crummy.

I've got that feeling back
Inside my tummy,
I need to go to the toilet
And I think it's runny!

Kerrie-Marie Snailham (10)
Hurst Knoll CE Primary School, Ashton-under-Lyne

YOU'RE SO GREAT

You're so great
You're so good,
You're so cool
You're so perfect.
You're so fab
You're the best,
Better than football itself.

You're *my* football boots!

Matthew Walker (10)
Hurst Knoll CE Primary School, Ashton-under-Lyne

MONSTERS

There're monsters in the wardrobe
There're monsters under the bed,
One jumped out of my closet
And *'Boo!'* it said.

These monsters live in towns,
In houses which are big
One ferocious monster jumped
And growled, *'Tig!'*

These monsters come in all sizes
Big, small, tall and thin
One jumped out as though being chased
Crash! Bang! Wallop!
Into the bin.

There's thunder in my room
Lots of loud sounds
All of the monsters
Boo! Tig! Crash! Bang! Wallop!
Had jumped, I found.

Jodie Mairs (9)
Longbarn Community Primary School, Warrington

BROTHER!

B   en is my brother
R   ussall is my dad
O   h, I love my brother
T   immy is my other brother
H   umatrude is my mum
E   verything is always a mess
R   ight now, I'm tidying up.

Rebecca Irwin (9)
Longbarn Community Primary School, Warrington

My Home Life

After school I go home and watch TV
In a bit, my friend would come to play out
We'll go to his house and play GTA.
He will say, 'Want sommert to eat?'
'Nar, I'm alright!' I would reply.
We'll play for an hour, taking turns
But then my dad will come to take me home.
Then I'll have my tea and go to a club
Band, band or swimming!
When I get back I do my homework (if not done)
And then go upstairs to put my PJs on
I'd go downstairs and watch TV
And then have a drink -
Then go back upstairs and go to sleep.

Matthew Conneely (9)
Longbarn Community Primary School, Warrington

School Poem

When I go to school,
I think it's a bit cruel.
People think it's boring
When in class, everybody's snoring.
Or when people are ill
The next day some children have a chill.

Talking and chattering
And when they are pattering.
When people are talking
Girls and boys are talking.

Ryan Larkin (10)
Longbarn Community Primary School, Warrington

I'M THE YOUNGEST . . .

I'm the youngest in the family
and nobody cares,
I'm the youngest in the family
and I hate *pears!*

I'm the youngest in the family
and the smallest too,
I'm the youngest in the family
And everyone tells me *what to do!*

I'm the youngest in the family
and I have a brother called Nick,
I'm the youngest in the family
and he makes me *sick!*

I'm the youngest in the family
and I have to go to school,
I'm the youngest in the family
and I would rather play *pool!*

I'm the youngest in the family
and I'm nine years old,
I'm the youngest in the family
and in the winter I am *cold!*

I'm the youngest in the family
and this is the end of my song,
I'm the youngest in the family
and I'm never wrong!

Gemma Woodward (9)
Longbarn Community Primary School, Warrington

MY MEMORY

I was going to my friend's house,
I was very excited.
I got in the car and I was off,
My mum said it was her birthday
And she'd got an electric car.

I got to my friend's house and
She waved at me,
I went into her garden and there it was,
The red and blue car,
She asked me if I wanted a go
And I said, 'Yes, please!'

I got on it and I was off,
Suddenly it came to a stop and
My friend said, 'Do you want a push?'
I said, 'Yes! But not too fast!'
But my friend pushed me really hard and
I fell down the kerb, cut my knee and banged my head.

I was crying really badly, so I went
To my mum and we went home.
I told my mum that I really
Liked that car, but my mum said that
I would never be going on that car again.
                                        I said, 'No!'

Molly Niklas (8)
Longbarn Community Primary School, Warrington

HALLOWE'EN

Hallowe'en is scary
Spiders are hairy
Witches with warts
Wearing large black coats.

Blue cats eating stinky rats
Fat bats eating small gnats,
On Hallowe'en you will see
The weirdest things you
Have ever seen.

The goblins dance and prance
The night away.
What a disgusting sight!

There are vampire cats
Eating people's hats.
Wizards are mixing
And as they're mixing,
They say, 'Double, double,
We are here for terrible trouble!'

Monstrous snails munching
Gigantic wails, dirty dogs
Eating big bad frogs.

Don't go out on Hallowe'en!

Saeed Ali (10)
Longshaw County Junior School, Blackburn

THE GHOST

It went to the pictures
It watched Men In Black II
It gave us all jobs
And then off it flew.

It went to the match
It went around the post
It started eating burgers
It was the little ghost.

Laura Robinson (9)
Longshaw County Junior School, Blackburn

THE TROPICAL ISLAND

On the tropical island
in the salty sea,
We'll see all the paradise
just you and me.

Look at the lemon
juicy and sour,
Eat the whole tree
they're ripe for an hour.

On the tropical island
in the salty sea,
We'll see all the paradise
just you and me.

Look at the mountains
surrounded by rocks,
If you go inside
you'll get chickenpox.

On the tropical island
in the salty sea,
We'll see all the paradise
just you and me.

Benjamin Walsh (8)
Longshaw County Junior School, Blackburn

MY MONSTER

My monster is bigger than -
The biggest skyscraper,
Taller than six hundred schools
And heavier than fourteen million pounds worth of houses.

My monster is fiercer than -
A ferocious panther,
Angrier than a raging bull
And wilder than a hurricane.

My monster is braver than -
Theseus and
Mightier than Zeus.

My monster is fitter than -
The fittest person
And faster than
The fastest Ferrari.

Daniel Brown (8)
Longshaw County Junior School, Blackburn

MY FRIEND REBBECA

R   uns fast
E   veryone is her friend
B   eautiful smile
B   eautiful face
E   veryone likes her
C   ares a lot
A   lways plays with me.

Anna-Lee Krause (8)
Longshaw County Junior School, Blackburn

DOLPHINS

Look into the dolphins' eyes
They're very shiny and gold.
They will not tell you any lies
Or little ones get told.

Smoothly swimming through the sea
Very good indeed.
They are very special and good to me
On their mum, they feed.

Through the shores and over rocky isles,
With the others too,
In the day, they swim some miles
They're a very dark blue.

I like all baby dolphins
They're very good and cute,
The king of all the seas
Calls them by a flute.

Tiffany Allan (10)
Longshaw County Junior School, Blackburn

WINTER POEM

W ailing winds and snow that destroys things
I n the darkness, ice appears.
N ight-time comes early, day is short
T rees are frozen.
E very day I like to play in the snow,
R acing like a Formula One car that chases winter away.

Liam Jackson (9)
Longshaw County Junior School, Blackburn

DAYDREAM

Miss Ravell thinks I'm reading,
But I'm really daydreaming,
Of swimming in the ocean,
Discovering shipwrecks and buried treasure.

Miss Ravell thinks I'm reading,
But I'm really daydreaming,
Of being on a tropical island,
Eating all the cheddar I could eat.

Miss Ravell thinks I'm reading,
But I'm really daydreaming,
Of exploring pyramids and discovering tombs
And Mummy's chasing me.

Teigan Kiss (8)
Longshaw County Junior School, Blackburn

THE SLEEPY HEDGEHOG

As winter is here, the spiky ball is sleeping
like he is dead,
The spiny snorter is curled up in his hole
in the oak tree,
The little brown hunter is not to be seen.

Now winter has gone, spring is here
The spiky ball is opening out.
Little chocolate button eyes open in a flash,
His first thought is of scrumptious beetles,
Juicy worms and crunchy earwigs
And he goes out hunting for them.

Matthew Leaver (10)
Longshaw County Junior School, Blackburn

THE THEME PARK

Welcome to the Theme Park!
The big wheel is like a spinning Jenny,
going round and round.
The echo of people screaming on the rides
The bright silver sparks from the Bumper Cars and
The thick smoke going up my nostrils.
Friends furiously fighting over food
With the smell of petrol, powering the rides.
I'm watching people throwing balls to win prizes
as the sizzling of burgers from the caravan, makes
my mouth water.
Parents shouting at their children and
The smell of salt and vinegar on my chips.
The rain trickling, as I walk down the
lonely narrow streets, on my way home.

Nathan Davis (11)
Longshaw County Junior School, Blackburn

MY MONSTER

My monster is greater than the Eiffel Tower
leaning down sideways.
Taller than Mount Everest,
Heavier than a million trucks,
stacked on top of each other.
My monster if fiercer than Zeus,
angrier than a raging tiger and
as strong as Arnold Schwarzenegger when
he's in action.
My monster is faster than Paula Radcliffe.

Ben Hodson (9)
Longshaw County Junior School, Blackburn

AUTUMN RISES

Autumn rises,
Eyes gently closed like a doll,
The tree mountaineer rests,
With a thoughtful soul,
The hibernation begins.
Many frights have drained him
Lots of depressions have floated away.
He can relax like a dead hedgehog.

Summer awakens,
His twilight eyes appear,
The fluffy roller has unrolled
Ready to have an exquisite meal.
The grass-pusher pushes
The beatle-scoffler scoffles,
The caterpillar-sniffler sniffles on to the concrete,
A stampede emerges,
Fluffy roller rolls,
Hedgehog, why?

Levi Katherine Mayman (11)
Longshaw County Junior School, Blackburn

NEIL

There was a young robot called Neil
Who liked to eat things made of steel,
Dessert was tinfoil
Which he washed down with oil,
Then he said, 'What a fabulous meal!'

Ethan Vernon (9)
Longshaw County Junior School, Blackburn

THE LONELY CHILD

Every day I arrive at school,
When I walk in the gates, everybody stares at me.
When I walk in the doors, I am lonely all day.
Only the teachers talk to me.

When it is break time, I am frightened,
I sit there on the bench, waiting to be picked for football.
Everyone is talking about a new girl starting our school,
She's in the playground, people make fun of her.

But why do they?
She slowly approaches me and takes her hood down.
She has dry, flaky skin, just like me.
She has eczema too.
We quickly become best friends.

Jonathan O'Neill (11)
Longshaw County Junior School, Blackburn

MY MONSTER

My monster is bigger than
the widest sea,
taller than the Eiffel Tower
and heavier than a ten ton truck.
My monster is fiercer than
a ferocious tiger,
angrier than a raging bull
and wilder than a hurricane.
My monster is braver than Hermes,
taller than Zeus and
heavier than the Minotaur.

Jodie-Mae Carter (8)
Longshaw County Junior School, Blackburn

THE HEDGEHOG

Hedgehogs eat slimy snails that slowly slither south.
Hedgehogs eat wet, wriggly worms that weirdly wriggle west.
Hedgehogs that are scared stiff crossing the stretched road
go into my back garden.
The hedgehog's velvety vest that is dragged along the floor.

The noisy eater plodding down the path and into my front garden.
It's the hedgehog silently moving.
The hedgehog's cute eyes as dark as the midnight sky.
It's now moving quietly from the old, cunning, sly fox.

D   ead silent, the fox moves forward,
A   nything could come to get you.
N   ever listen to that sly old fox,
G   et away quick, it's behind you,
E   ating your little bugs,
R   un away back home little hedgehog.

Stephanie Szejner (10)
Longshaw County Junior School, Blackburn

DAYDREAMS

Miss Ravell thinks I'm reading, but really
I am driving a sports car.

Miss Ravell thinks I'm reading, but really
I am playing football.

Miss Ravell thinks I'm reading, but I am
really pretending that I'm playing out
in the snow.

Ryan Dean (8)
Longshaw County Junior School, Blackburn

I'M IN THE MOOD FOR FOOD

I'm in the mood,
I'm desperate for food,
It is joyous to me,
I want something for tea,
I could eat anything of course,
So get me a king-size horse,
I want a drink of red wine,
At least something that dribbles down my spine.

I'm in the mood,
I'm desperate for food,
My belly is starting to rumble,
I'm about to tumble.

I looked in my kitchen
My food was finally there,
In a stew of rabbit hair.

Josh Alston (9)
Longshaw County Junior School, Blackburn

MY MONSTER

My monster is wider than
Trafalgar Square
Bigger than twenty houses
And heavier than the Iron Man.

My monster is the hero
Of the world,
He has big glowing, red eyes
And curling green teeth.

Nyle Shepherd (8)
Longshaw County Junior School, Blackburn

I'M SICK OF ANIMALS

I once saw a little ant,
Lying in my plant.
It likes a rabbit,
It has a habit,
I'm sick of little ants.

I once saw a funny dog,
Sitting on a log.
It likes a frog,
It sat on a hog,
I'm sick of funny dogs.

I once saw a fat lion,
Playing with an iron.
It loves reaping,
I'm going crazy, it's leaping,
I'm really sick of fat lions.

Aafira Gani (8)
Longshaw County Junior School, Blackburn

MY MONSTER

My monster is bigger than Russia
Taller than Blackpool Tower
And heavier than a ten tonne truck.

My monster is madder than a mad scientist
Angrier than a tiger
And wilder than a lion.

My monster is fatter than Henry VIII
My monster is a grumpy monster.

Nathanial Shaw (8)
Longshaw County Junior School, Blackburn

DAYDREAMS

Miss Ravell thinks I'm reading
But really I am daydreaming
I am thinking that I am walking
Along in the land of wonders, singing along.

Miss Ravell thinks I'm listening
But really I am daydreaming
I am flying around with fairies
We are giving pounds to children.

Miss Ravell thinks I am watching
But really I am daydreaming
I am in Willy Wonka's chocolate factory
Eating all the chocolate and candy I want.

Rachel Quigley (9)
Longshaw County Junior School, Blackburn

WITCHES' MAGIC SPELL

Bubble, bubble, toil and trouble,
Fire burns and cauldron bubbles.
Fillet of toad with a slimy tongue
And it might be very wrong
But add the leg of an evil bat
And the tail of a flea-ridden cat.
Eyes of a cow, toes of ten pigs,
Wool of sheep, a string of figs,
Mix in the shell of a crab.
Then the remains of a kebab.
For a charm of powerful trouble
Like a hell-broth, boil and bubble.

Zoe Lloyd (11)
Longshaw County Junior School, Blackburn

WHEN YOU COME INTO THE GRAVEYARD

When you come into the graveyard,
You better beware,
Because the zombie is somewhere.

When you come into the graveyard,
Please, please don't, please don't boast,
Because you'll see an angry ghost.

When you come into the graveyard,
Don't despair,
Because the spooks don't really care.

When you come into the graveyard,
Don't do any voodoo,
Because everything will come after you.

Daniel Bond (11)
Longshaw County Junior School, Blackburn

SPIKY THE HEDGEHOG

He has dozed all winter, he curls out of a ball,
He's soft and cuddly, he's very small.
He goes scurrying about for slugs and snails
And as he walks, you can't see his tail.
He's got thousands of spikes,
You couldn't catch him on a bike!
He goes out hunting in the night,
Little hedgehog, watch out for a fright!
A little spiky ball, rolling on the floor,
Bye-bye little hedgehog, as there's a mighty roar.

Why did Spiky cross the road?

Liam Wright (10)
Longshaw County Junior School, Blackburn

MY POEM OF COLOURS

Yellow is golden sand, smooth beneath my feet,
A shiny cheque in the bank,
My freshly made lemon juice,
The burning flames, dancing in the fire.

Green is a school form letter for bad behaviour,
Or mint ice cream dripping down by the sides of my mouth.
Rustling leaves falling from a tree
Bright crunchy pears in a bowl.

Orange is a bright, delicious fruit,
Or a deserted island, bathed in a hot sun,
A healthy, crunchy carrot, ready to be eaten,
A sleek tiger, hunting its prey.

Black is the night sky with twinkling stars,
A gleaming cat in the road,
Elliott's cool brand new school bag,
The class' shiny leather shoes.

Jasmine Marsh (10)
Longshaw County Junior School, Blackburn

I CAN DREAM OF A . . .

I can dream of a flower
I can dream of a strawberry that's very sour
I can dream of a chocolate sundae
I can dream of a fry-up on Monday
I can dream of Rovers winning
I can dream of going swimming
Splash!
I wake up wet!

Lauren Sheppard (9)
Longshaw County Junior School, Blackburn

A SMALL QUARREL

He didn't bring me a packet of sweets like usual,
I stood with someone else in the line.

I stood waiting for him to go to choir
He went outside to play football.

He left me to play his guitar
I went to play the violin.

I kicked the ball at him,
He tripped me up.

He ripped my paper in half,
I drew a face on his.

I gave him a funny look
He called me a nasty name.

He pulled my hair hard,
I thumped him even harder.

I walked home with him,
He slept at my house.

Callum Pearson (11)
Longshaw County Junior School, Blackburn

MY FRIEND ANNA-LEE

My friend Anna-Lee has a beautiful smile
My friend Anna-Lee has long hair
My friend Anna-Lee she is tall
My friend Anna-Lee she wears glasses
My friend Anna-Lee she always wears her uniform.

Rebecca Burns (8)
Longshaw County Junior School, Blackburn

THE PIZZA

I'm making a pizza for tea
there'll be some for you and
some for me.

I'll throw on the tail of a rat
I'll throw in a wing of a bat
I'll squeeze out some carrot juice,
and give you a chocolate mousse.

I'm making pizza for tea
there'll be some for you and
some for me.

I'll slap on some cauliflower
I'll turn you into a lovely flower
I'll put you in my car and
take you to a French bar.

I'm making a pizza for tea
there'll be some for you and
some for me!

Holly Mayo (8)
Longshaw County Junior School, Blackburn

A WITCH'S BREW

Dogs' tails, French snails,
Slimy toads and frogs,
Mouldy water, men of slaughter,
Hairy cats and dogs.
Abracadabra, walla-kazam
Make this witch's brew go *bam!*

Melissa Shah (9)
Longshaw County Junior School, Blackburn

WHAT MY DAD IS LIKE

I like my dad
He's like a PlayStation pad
He teases the dog
Jumps like a frog
Gets a fiver in the mail
Puts the Sega up for sale
He overtakes a bus
But he never makes a fuss
He'll kick a ball
But never fall
He's never in a mood
But he eats good food
Because he's my dad.

Joseph Walsh (10)
Longshaw County Junior School, Blackburn

IMAGINARY FRIENDS

I have a friend
who isn't there
in fact she isn't anywhere!

My friend is imaginary
or so Mum says
yet I see her now.

She sits right next to me
at tea and when
I watch TV.

Lauren Nixon (8)
Longshaw County Junior School, Blackburn

SCHOOL IS CLOSED TODAY BECAUSE . . .

The geography teacher got lost
The history teacher had a date
The RE teacher had a different religion
The cookery teacher married the dough
The science teacher blew a fuse
The art teacher glued himself to the chair
The PE teacher wasn't fit enough for the job
The music teacher died in songs
The drama teacher couldn't stop dancing
The maths teacher went to calculations world
The woodwork teacher got a splinter
The French teacher couldn't understand English
And the English teacher was written.

Samantha Allan (10)
Longshaw County Junior School, Blackburn

MY MONSTER

My monster is greater than a skyscraper
He is stronger than eight sharks
put together
My monster weighs, allegedly, over
five hundred pounds.
He is longer than two bedrooms.
My monster is better than
Superman himself.
He is the best I think.
My monster is wider than a vineyard.

Michael Loadwick (9)
Longshaw County Junior School, Blackburn

MY MONSTER

My monster's scary,
He's taller than a house
My monster's cuddly and
Snug as a mouse.

He is so kind and he is
So sweet, he does the washing
And he folds it so neat.
When I'm in the bath
He tickles my toes,
When he's asleep,
I tickle his nose.
When he's awake, he
Kisses my nose.

I love my monster, his name is Lee,
Everyone should have a monster -
Just like me!

Christopher Pemberton (9)
Longshaw County Junior School, Blackburn

DAYDREAMS

Miss Ravell thinks I'm reading
But really I am dreaming that I am floating
On a paradise island with lots of fruit.

Miss Ravell thinks I'm reading
But really I am dreaming that I am flying
In the sky on a dragon.

Ashley Dean (8)
Longshaw County Junior School, Blackburn

THE NOISY SONG

The sausages go *sizzle, sizzle*
The bees go *buzz, buzz*
The people in bed go *zzz, zzz*
The doors go *bang, bang*
The wind goes *whoosh, whoosh*
The water goes *splash, splash*
The cork goes *pop, pop*
The bottles go *smash, smash*
The lolly is *crackling, crackling*
You get a great big *crack, crack*
The cars go *vroom, vroom*
The vans go *crash, crash*
The powers go *zap, zap*.

Laura Linley (10)
Longshaw County Junior School, Blackburn

MY MONSTER

My monster is taller than the Eiffel Tower
He's stronger than eight gorillas.
He's faster than a missile and six cheetahs.
He's heavier than six grizzly bears
He's wilder than a tornado and
An earthquake.
He's scarier than a vampire,
He's ten times better than Spider-Man
And he's very famous.
He's the best, he's my best friend,
I think he's called Ben.

Arif Patel (9)
Longshaw County Junior School, Blackburn

THE SEASONS

It is winter now,
The cold and windy season,
Where it rains a lot
And blows all the leaves down.

It is spring now,
The sunny a lot and leafy season,
It rains a lot less now
And leaves are growing.

It is summer now,
A hot and sunny season,
It hardly rains now,
I never get wet.

It is autumn now,
The cold and leaf dying season.
It's starting to rain now
And blows the leaves down.

Ricky Harvey (10)
Longshaw County Junior School, Blackburn

DAYDREAMS

Miss Ravell thinks I'm reading,
But really I am inside a picture.
The picture is of a beautiful paradise,
With a rainbow over my head.

Miss Ravell thinks I'm reading,
But really I am daydreaming.
I am in a golden castle filled with jewels,
With lots and lots of money.

Miss Ravell thinks I'm reading,
But really I am daydreaming.
I am on a tropical island,
With an ice lolly and a beautiful pool.

Miss Ravell thinks I'm reading,
But really I am daydreaming.
I am in a chocolate world,
Which is so yummy.

Coral Duckworth (9)
Longshaw County Junior School, Blackburn

EVERYTHING'S LOVELY

One day I went to a park
    It was lovely
I made my very own ark
    It was lovely
I saw a little bird
    It was lovely
I saw a spotty leopard
    It was lovely
I've been collecting shells
    It was lovely
I've been playing with my bells
    It was lovely
I played for Man U
    It was lovely
I played with my friend Lauren
    It was lovely! Lovely! Lovely!
Lovely!

Melissa Nelson (8)
Longshaw County Junior School, Blackburn

OVER THE WHOLE WORLD

What is that, that I can see
Over the mountains, over the hills,
Over the houses, over the bays
Over you and over me?

Twinkle, twinkle as they call out
As night comes by
And as soon as the morning light shines
They vanish into the deep blue sky.

Tanmona Ahmed (10)
Longshaw County Junior School, Blackburn

WHAT I LIKE

I like being funny
but I'm always very hungry.
I like drawing,
I also like things glowing.
I like English
and I'm nowhere near foolish.
I like living
I like giving as well.
I'm happy 'cause I've got friends and family.

Heidi Forster (8)
Longshaw County Junior School, Blackburn

MY EVIL DEVIL

My evil devil is as hot as molten lava
He is as big as the two towers
Its teeth are as sharp as blades
It is as strong as a fire-breathing dragon
Made out of metal

It's faster than a jet-packed cheetah
It's scarier than a ghost
My evil devil is always bloodthirsty
He is always ready for battle.
His name is Scorch.

Cameron Barker (9)
Longshaw County Junior School, Blackburn

MY BABY BROTHER IS A KILLER!

My baby brother is a killer,
He pulls my hair,
Spits in my face,
Then throws me down on the floor,
He takes off my glasses,
Then tries them on,
Then throws them away,
Bites my toes,
My mum says, 'Get off the floor.'

Billie-Jo Holden (8)
Longshaw County Junior School, Blackburn

MY MONSTER

My monster is larger than a million houses put together.
He is fluffier than ten white wolves.
He is heavier than five blue whales.
His eyes are like the deep blue sea shimmering away.
My monster is the loveliest monster in the world.

Janine Westwell (8)
Longshaw County Junior School, Blackburn

ALIENS ARE COMING

What was that?
It's coming closer,
Quick let's run.
Aliens are no fun
They're coming to get us.
Who wants to play hide-and-seek?
We can hide
They can seek.
Hey, look over there
Aliens are everywhere.
They found us out too.

Joel Alston (9)
Longshaw County Junior School, Blackburn

MY MONSTER

My monster is bigger than the highest mountain,
Taller than the tallest tower in the world
And heavier than the white whale.

My monster is fiercer than Medusa from the Greek myths,
Angrier than an atrocious lion
And wilder than a wild boar.

My monster is braver than Theseus, mightier than Zeus,
Faster than an aeroplane,
Fitter than a kangaroo.

Mathew Oddie (8)
Longshaw County Junior School, Blackburn

THE HUNGRY HEDGEHOG

'Mummy there's a hedgehog in the garden,
He's gobbling up the cat's food
Now he's caught a snail and is eating that too.
Crunch! There goes the shell . . . *Eeeeeeewwww!*

Mummy there's a hedgehog in the garden,
He's digging up the soil with his claws,
Now he's caught a worm and is eating it like spaghetti,
There goes the head . . . *Ouch!*

Mummy there's a hedgehog in the garden,
He's found a group of beetles,
They're all running away,
He's too fast, he's got one . . . *Crunch!*

Mummy there's a hedgehog in the garden,
He's snatched a millipede from its leaf,
He's grubbling it down,
It's all gone . . . *Goooowwww!*

Mummy there's a hedgehog in the garden,
He's bristle-balling, he's heard something!
Oh no! It's the cat!
Ha! Ha! The tabby's playing football with him.

Mummy, the hedgehog is running away,
He's dropped down a rabbit hole,
Oh no!
Mummy, he's asleep!'

Benjamin Baron (11)
Longshaw County Junior School, Blackburn

THE HEDGEHOG POEM

The long spikes bursting out,
See the hedgehog stretching like a bobble.
He's off on a long journey,
His spikes are deep, dark brown, like chocolate
And his chubby cheeks are like marshmallows.
There he goes, looking for food.

When he's finished, he walks up the hill
With his tiny leather padded feet.
Once back home, he curls up in a ball
His dark spikes, like a hairbrush
And his cosy strawberry belly, is all nice and warm.
His tail's not showing. Where can it be?
His colourful eyes are shining down
As he gets up and off he goes again.

Lindsey Barton (10)
Longshaw County Junior School, Blackburn

ISABEL

Isabel met a wolf who was devious
Isabel thought he looked mischievous
The wolf was nasty, the wolf was smelly
He wanted Isabel in his belly
The wolf said, 'Isabel come home with me,
Cos I'm going to eat you for my tea.'
Isabel, Isabel didn't worry
Isabel didn't scream or scurry
She poured him out a poisoned cuppa
Then Isabel took him home for *her* supper.

Dominick Jeal (11)
Longshaw County Junior School, Blackburn

DAD IS THE BEST

D ad makes me happy
A nd is always there for me
D ad is great at making me a brilliant cup of tea.

I love my dad
S o much

T hat if he wasn't my dad I would want him to meet me.
H ave fun is what we always do
E xcept when I go to the loo.

B rilliant smile
E very day
S its down when he doesn't want
T o play.

I love my dad!

James Archer (9)
Neston Primary School, Neston

WILL THERE BE . . .

When I grow old, will the grass still be green?
Will the birds fly about or will they be unseen?
Will people still rant, rave and shout?
Will lions and tigers chase people about?
Will there be houses or will there be huts?
Will people still have bad grazes and cuts?
Will there still be a PlayStation 2,
Or will a genius invent something new?
Will the ants be as small as can be?
I don't know, let's wait and see.

Roberto Whitley (10)
Neston Primary School, Neston

A MEADOW

The meadow is a mellow cat,
Small and frail.
Lolling about, sleeping in the breeze.
With her soothing purr and pointed ears.
Hour upon hour she dreams
The swaying, hypnotic grass,
Dandelions tickling her ears.
her eyes flutter,
She licks her pads
And when the seeds disperse
She lumbers up to her feet
Shakes the pollen to the ground,
She purrs and mews with leisure.
But on cold nights,
When the grass doesn't play its tune
You can see her, calm and still
Crying in the morning dew.

William Flaherty (11)
Neston Primary School, Neston

IN MY BOX
(Based on 'The Magic Box' by Kit Wright)

In my box I would have . . .
A caring word to say,
In the darkest shadow, evil waits
And a king-size pack of After Eights,
A dazzling, golden sunset,
A moment in time I won't regret,
Held together with the four elements.

Martin Hannam (11)
Neston Primary School, Neston

BOOK

As I turn the front cover,
The title says,
'The Mysterious Book of
Strange Stories'.

Then I turn to the story,
Turning pages as I read,
Coming to the centre,
Loving every word.

Coming to the end,
Always hoping to keep it going,
Then I come to the last page,
Reading every word and phrase.

Then I close the back cover
And go over the whole story.

Stephen Daley (11)
Neston Primary School, Neston

DESCRIPTIVE POEM

Their fur as warm as a boiler
Their fierce eyes staring, looking for prey
As they wait in suspense to pounce
Their paws moving slowly in the dead of the night.

Their black and ginger fur disguised
In the fallen leaves of the trees
Their claws as sharp as a knife
Ready to scratch their prey.

Daniel Stone (11)
Neston Primary School, Neston

WHAT I'LL PUT IN MY POCKET FOR SCHOOL

I will put . . .
A broken pencil,
A piece of pizza,
A sharp compass,
A ball of bubblegum,
A catapult,
A couple of stones,
A video game,
A bouncy ball
And a pea-shooter
That's what I'll put in my pocket for school.

Ryan Butterworth (10)
Neston Primary School, Neston

WHAT WILL I PUT IN MY JUNIOR WIZARD KIT?

I will put in . . .
A toad with decrepit butterfly wings.
The head of the gorgon Medusa.
A snapped and crooked wand.
A human sacrifice with a sticking out bone.
A black and rusty cauldron.
A group of lizards' legs.
The sharpest, scariest lion's teeth.
A book of secret dark art
And a laboratory of the creepiest things.

Steven Barnes-Smith (9)
Neston Primary School, Neston

THE WORLD IS IN MY PLATE

The broccoli trees loom over my plate,
Potatoes just like rocks,
Peas like mini footballs
And carrots look like logs.

Ice cream sundae mountain,
With cherry boulders on top,
Vanilla, strawberry, chocolate,
Washed down with fizzy pop.

Battered cod plateau,
Skyscrapers are my chips,
Mushy peas are stinking swamps,
Passing through my lips.

Crunchy bread and soup,
Are my rivers, streams and lakes,
The buildings and the houses,
Are my tasty cream cakes.

Marshmallow trampolines,
Squelchy mashed potato,
Sugar for a salty beach,
My sun's a red tomato.

The spinach is my jungle,
Orange juice is my sea,
My plate can be a world,
But really it's my tea!

Daniel Barraclough (11)
Neston Primary School, Neston

EXTREMES!

The rain slashed down like a beating of a drum,
The wind howled around hissing, 'Come, come!'
The snow set an icy spell freezing all the streams
The streets were all quiet and empty, hiding from the extremes.
Then, on a sunny, summer's day our friend the sun came out to play.

Amy Milton (11)
Neston Primary School, Neston

SCHOOL

S   omewhere in school today you will find children,
C   hildren in the playground, children inside,
H   ome time comes, children run to get out,
O   ut they go to meet their mums,
O   ur teachers go for a drink,
L   aughs and jokes for a while, then home at last.

Dean Meadows (11)
Neston Primary School, Neston

DESCRIPTION

The fur is orange, black and white
The orange fur is as orange as a fire
The tongue is as red as a bright red bobble
The tiger walks along the leaves that have fallen to the floor.

Charlotte Morgan (11)
Neston Primary School, Neston

AUTUMN DAYS

The sun was a shining spotlight,
Among the freshening breeze,
The sea was a lovely shade of blue,
Near the chestnut trees.

The sky was glittering in my eyes,
As clouds sailed by,
The grass was as green as peppermint,
As the whirling wind cried.

The ocean held its secrets,
As willow trees swayed,
As the orange leaves fell,
In the autumn days.

Bethni Maylor (11)
Neston Primary School, Neston

THE INVISIBLE BEAST!

The invisible beast is stalking through the woods
but though you cannot see him, he can see you very well
When he sees you coming he will crack the branches
But you can't see him even when it is light
He is as green as a tree so you will never see him
Not even a mouse, he is nearly as big as a house.

He sounds like a lion or even like an alien
He lives in the pale branches
His teeth are as sharp as razor blades
He will eat you in a second
He loves little girls and boys on leaves
You will never know where he is
But though you cannot see him, he can see you very well.

Danielle Reading (9)
Ormskirk CE Primary School, Ormskirk

THE VISIBLE BEAST

My beast has large red eyes
And people think he eats pies.
His feet are bumpy and blue,
Watch out he might eat you.
My beast moves like a cheetah
And he calls himself Peter.
He can run a mile
And he goes on trial.

My beast lives in a haunted cave
Near a spooky grave.
This is a large cave
You must be brave.
He speaks Scottish
And his mouth is spottish.
He always groans
And always moans.

My beast eats flesh
And is put behind mesh.
He could eat a shark
And makes a spark.
My beast eats his food, *gobble, gobble, gulp!*
Before that he beats it to a pulp.
He dips it into curry
Then they worry.

Aimee Reeves (8)
Ormskirk CE Primary School, Ormskirk

THE VISIBLE BEAST

She has one giant eye in her head,
Her hair is as golden as gold.
She has one big antennae which always turns red
And she smells like mould.
She gallops as fast as a horse
And likes to eat hot sauce.
Although she is fast
She can't catch you if you hide.

She lives in a cave
And meets her mum in a grave.
She's very brave
To throw a rave.
She speaks Greek
Out of her cheek.
But although she is fast
She can't catch you if you hide.

She eats you whole
On a thin pole.
She will eat you as loud as she can
But she will never eat a pan.
She will eat branches and fat juicy men
She will eat a big juicy hen.
But although she is fast,
She can't catch you if you hide.

Laura Caunce (9)
Ormskirk CE Primary School, Ormskirk

THE VISIBLE BEAST

He has 15 claws on each hand
And 20 toes on each foot
He has two tiny heads
And his eyes are black as soot
He moves very slowly at daytime
But at night exceedingly fast
He tries his hardest to catch you
'Cause his belly is huge and vast.

He lives in the dark, dingy sewers
He's lonely there as well
He doesn't like being on his own
But there's no one he will tell
He growls a breathtaking growl
It's been more scary in the past
He tries his hardest to catch you
'Cause his belly is huge and vast.

He eats fat, tempting children
And enormous lions, although
He doesn't like the food he eats
He likes gingerbread men made of dough
He rips off the skin bit by bit
We'll see of you the last
He tries his hardest to catch you
'Cause his belly is huge and vast.

Natasha McDonnell (9)
Ormskirk CE Primary School, Ormskirk

THE VISIBLE BEAST

He has pointy fingernails
And has a dozen tails
He is purple and blue
And full of goo.
He always makes fun of other's height
And goes to bed at midnight
You may like him
Because he loves you.

He lives in a dustbin
And always has a nasty grin
He likes to speak German and French
And every day he smashes a bench
He wants to live in a tree
Because then he will smile with glee
You may like him
Because he loves you.

When he eats his food he twirls
And he eats little girls
He likes to eat big things
Such as dustbins
He likes to eat loud
As loud as a tractor making a field ploughed
You may like him
Because he loves you.

Christopher Whitehurst (9)
Ormskirk CE Primary School, Ormskirk

THE VISIBLE BEAST

His belly really fat
He has horns as sharp as a rhino
And has a pet cat
His skin as green spring grass
Eyes as big as a house
Ears as big as a door
Although he is visible
But it seems he's invisible.

He speaks like a cat
He lives in a spooky attic
He screams like a bat
He sleeps in cobwebs
He's got a bit of an American accent
His voice is as loud as the army firing guns
Although he is visible
But it seems he's invisible.

He eats with his toes
He eats elephants as big as Blackpool Tower
Sometimes he'll eat with his nose
He eats with lots of wood
He eats little girls
Also he eats chairs
Although he is visible
But it seems he is invisible.

Ben Williams
Ormskirk CE Primary School, Ormskirk

THE INVISIBLE BEAST

The cellar that it lives in is dark, damp and cold
And if anyone steps near it
It gobbles them and they're gone forever
You can hear its deep hisses
From down in the dark cellar
Its sparkly purple fangs
And all its purple eyes
Like a curled up blanket.

The flap of its wings
Like the beat of a drum
Always flapping
Ringing in your ears
Its sharp indigo claws
Will tear you to pieces
It comes out of its lair . . .

Its pale blue claws
As thin as a stick
Its purple twirls are dotted all over
Right, left and everywhere
It swoops about like an owl
Its long hair flowing in the wind
Indigo and blue
It is extremely scary!

Emily Temple (9)
Ormskirk CE Primary School, Ormskirk

THE VISIBLE BEAST

The beast that is visible
Has an oval-shaped head.
He shows his sharp, metal teeth
As he sleeps in his bed.
His arms and legs are sticks
And he can camouflage himself
In a bush that pricks.
He moves fast and swiftly
Like a bird in flight.
But although he is visible
You never know where he is.

It lives in the bottom of a deep, smelly swamp
With leeches, snakes and things.
Down to the swamp
His food he brings
His voice is a low, screeching sound
Like a car hitting the brakes.
But although he is visible
You never know where he is.

He eats whatever gets in his way
Including things that are huge.
But if it's something that he doesn't like
He'll cover it in gunge.
It swallows its food with a loud gulp
And although it sounds disgusting
He'll eat it when it's dusty
But although it's visible
You never know where it is.

Jade Forshaw (9)
Ormskirk CE Primary School, Ormskirk

THE VISIBLE BEAST

The visible beast is ferocious
It has teeth that gleam like pearls.
It has seven long legs,
Its favourite food is little girls.
It speaks a weird language.
It has seven flat toes
Even though it's not invisible
You can't see it everywhere it goes.

The beast is ferocious
It will make you squirm
It hides in wardrobes
And makes you wish
You never took that wrong turn
It speaks with a tube
And has seven flat toes
Even though it's not invisible
You can't see it everywhere it goes.

The beast is quick
And graceful
Very quick.
Nobody is more paceful
Its fur is prickly
And when it sees girls
He thinks they are his foes
Even though it's not invisible
You can't see it everywhere it goes.

Thomas Clegg (9)
Ormskirk CE Primary School, Ormskirk

THE INVISIBLE BEAST

The beast that is invisible
Has an orange face
His eyes are kind of creepy
His feet are made of lace
If you are not careful
You will be in his bowl

He moves very slow
He likes the gentle blow
He has tiny blue wings which flap about
You will have to be careful or he will eat you
He is closer every second
He eats children and adults too.

He watches every move you make
He is a useless beast
He says how long does it take
He doesn't like visitors
He doesn't like animals
How mean is he
His legs are as heavy as cannonballs.

Bethanie Spears (8)
Ormskirk CE Primary School, Ormskirk

THE INVISIBLE BEAST

If you go down to the swamp one night
When it's gloomy and dark,
You might hear some whispering
From down inside the park.
Then crunching like a lion eating up his prey
But deep inside the forest where nobody goes
He'll be there someday.

Tonight's the night when he searches for his prey.
So if you go out, beware the invisible beast might be about.
So be careful when you're out and about
On your own.

Lauren Gaunt
Ormskirk CE Primary School, Ormskirk

THE VISIBLE BEAST

He has one massive eye,
So that he can spy.
He has an enormous square head
And if you show him your fear, he will give you a nasty sigh.
And he never ever lies down on his dirty bed,
But he runs as fast as a cheetah,
So run as fast as you can.

He lives in a cave
And he always puts on a rave.
Also he is very, very brave
And whenever he is asleep he hears a wave.
Even though he's brave he always gets a crave,
Also he speaks Spanish so no one can tell what he's saying.
But he runs as fast as a cheetah,
So run as fast as you can.

He eats with a wide mouth
And keeps his grain.
Also he gets a horrible pain,
He loves girls.
That were lovely pearls
And his favourite is hair as golden as a coin
But he runs as fast as a cheetah
So run as fast as you can.

Abigail Bentley (8)
Ormskirk CE Primary School, Ormskirk

THE VISIBLE BEAST

The beast that is visible is dark and blue
You better be careful in case it gets you.
It has sharp red eyes
And you'll think it spies.
For everywhere it goes
It can see you.

Although it hates toys
It likes little boys.
It moves like a chicken
But will give you a good kicking.
For everywhere it goes
It can see you.

It lives in a mountain
Misty and wide.
Some people say it has a loop
Down the side.
For everywhere it goes
It can see you.

Clare Grayson (9)
Ormskirk CE Primary School, Ormskirk

THE INVISIBLE BEAST

The beast that is invisible
Is coming to your house
It is walking past your neighbours
As quiet as a mouse
As he barks and hisses
He still has that stinky smell
As you look behind your curtain
He stares and glares at you very well.

He likes to eat little children
And tall adults too
As he looks at you he'll probably be saying
Moo, moo
He has purple horns and a nose ring too
He likes to put on purple gel
As you look behind your curtain
He stares and glares at you very well.

Eloise Cottam
Ormskirk CE Primary School, Ormskirk

THE VISIBLE BEAST

With every step it's getting closer
So run as fast as you can.
He is as hairy as a gorilla
He speaks like a man.
So watch out, he's coming to get you
If he can.

With every step it's getting closer
So run as fast as you can.
He lives down a giant, abandoned toilet
He speaks like a cartoon van.
So watch out, he's coming to get you
If he can.

With every step it's getting closer
So run as fast as you can.
He eats rubbish out of slimy wheelie bins
He eats like a nan.
So watch out, he's coming to get you
If he can.

Megan Judge
Ormskirk CE Primary School, Ormskirk

THE INVISIBLE BEAST

My fierce invisible beast
His teeth are as sharp as saws
His toenails are sticky out
And his tummy is as big as a ball
Big sharp teeth that can kill you with one chew
He is multicoloured
His horns are bright blue.

His face is as orange as a tangerine
He has green eyes
They look very evil
His teeth are very yellow and they don't look nice
He only likes metal things to eat
He never closes his mouth
So you can see what he is eating
It doesn't matter what's inside it.

Lauren Nixon (8)
Ormskirk CE Primary School, Ormskirk

THE INVISIBLE BEAST

The beast that is invisible
Has very sharp teeth
He could rip you up into shreds
You will not want to meet him
Because you will turn into stone
He will grab you and tear off your flesh
He's got eyes as red as scarlet
His teeth are as mouldy as sweets.

He lives in the swamps in a very big cave
You will notice he is in because you will hear him
If you walk into his cave you will tread on bones
If you are lucky you will be alive
He has horns as sharp as knives
And ears that are good
He will hiss at you
Everyone is scared of him.

Daniel Bailie (8)
Ormskirk CE Primary School, Ormskirk

THE INVISIBLE BEAST

The beast that is a hunchback
Is howling through the park
You don't know when it's coming
Though it's very, very dark
You spy its crooked outline
You can spy on his footprints to see where they lead
But if you want to live well keep your needs.

His name no one knows
To his feet to his toes
He rips and skips some rather off-meals
And he charges over fields
He makes rather gory deals
And rips up wheels
He snacks on seals
And that will be the end of you.

Luke Hardman (9)
Ormskirk CE Primary School, Ormskirk

THE INVISIBLE BEAST

His horns are large and pointy and very, very sharp
His tail is short and spiky
And he's stalking you through the park
His three legs are manky
And his bones will scare you off
He lives in a damp, dirty quarry
You should have listened to your mum
Now you're feeling sorry.

His footsteps are growing louder
But you cannot see it
He will swallow you whole
If he gets a chance to hit
So listen to me now, don't go back out there
Because he is worse than just a grizzly bear
He has six eyes on his head
He will whack you with his tail
But he does not care.

James MacGregor (9)
Ormskirk CE Primary School, Ormskirk

THE INVISIBLE BEAST

The beast that is invisible
Has dark scarlet eyes
With green gungy feet
It loves and loves bone pies
With lots of blood sauce too
And if you ever met it
You'd turn to gungy goo!

He has eyes everywhere
So you better watch out
With its shiny white teeth
And horns that stick out
So if it's feeling peckish
This is a warning
Because you might be gone by the morning!

Catherine Elliott (8)
Ormskirk CE Primary School, Ormskirk

ORKS

Orks are bad
But never sad
They live on Mars
And always see the stars
They like to fight
Mostly at night
They eat like animals
And might even be cannibals.

Orks play drums
But they don't eat buns
Some orks are tall
But, they don't play with a ball
Their skin is green
And their hands are like a bean
Orks are fat
And that is that.

Syd McAllister (9)
Ormskirk CE Primary School, Ormskirk

THE INVISIBLE BEAST

There is a very hairy monster
He is walking through the park
He has three eyes and a large pointy nose
Fangs coming from his mouth with blood dripping down
He has a dark brown body with very slimy hands
His cave is very gloomy with slimy walls and it's wet
It's very wide and deep with very lumpy rocks on the top
Also it's very, very dark.

It gobbles up its food and rips it up in his mouth
It looks for children all around
It moves quickly and slowly
It eats children up and all kinds of insects
It speaks loudly and snores very quietly
It hides behind bushes and trees.

Nicola Souther (9)
Ormskirk CE Primary School, Ormskirk

FOOTBALL

'Uuu!' goes a shout
Through the middle and out
There's a goal from Patrick
Yaaa, he scored a hat-trick
What position does he play?
It doesn't matter anyway
Defender, striker, midfielder
Ask the coach, he says, 'Oh yeah!'
He hit it in the back of the net
'Oh yes,' yells the coach, 'I've won that bet.'

Kelly Henderson (11)
Pooltown Community Junior School, Ellesmere Port

AUTUMN

Autumn has come, the wind starts blowing,
As the cold cat's eyes are glowing.
Not many people are walking on the streets and sidewalks,
As the rustling leaves are chattering.

The thunder and lightning seizes the grass,
The wind and lightning breaks the glass.
Along comes the blizzard with its ice-cold flakes,
They look like icing off a cake.

The thunder and lightning strikes from the sky
Like a war plane trying to fly.

When the fog strikes you in your car,
You can't see very far.
When the dew wets the grass,
The great see-through liquid spreads.

Nathan Reid (11)
Pooltown Community Junior School, Ellesmere Port

TIGER

Tigers have bloody teeth
Don't go near them, they give you grief
Turtles are a yummy dish
Followed by a big fat fish
Tigers are not that sweet
'Cause their favourite food is human meat
Argh look, a rabbit I see
I think tiger caught her dad for tea!

Toni Harvey (10)
Pooltown Community Junior School, Ellesmere Port

MY AUTUMN POEM

The autumn brings
a howling wind.

The trees blush as their leaves
drift off down the street.

The rain gurgles in the grid.

The autumn brings a furious rain
as it bangs on my windowpane.

Leanne Ackroyd (11)
Pooltown Community Junior School, Ellesmere Port

THE AUTUMN

In the autumn, crispy leaves lie upon the floor.
In the autumn, the whistling wind knocks on your door.
In the autumn, kids kick leaves everywhere.
In the autumn, the wind blows your hair anywhere.
You can catch a cold, but your washing finds it hard to hold.
The trees whine, when the wind passes by.

Cheryl Glover (11)
Pooltown Community Junior School, Ellesmere Port

THE BEDROOMS

My bedroom is small,
Posters are covered on my wall.
I play music all day,
I have loads to say.

My mum and dad's room is big,
My mum wears a wig.
My dad likes sport,
He plays on the tennis court.

Terri Casey Golden (11)
Pooltown Community Junior School, Ellesmere Port

THE PERSON CREEPER

They go where they don't want to go
They hang from the ceiling and they crawl down low
He moves to escape from the room
But ouch, he's been killed by a cloth or a broom
His life was very quick and short
He was once one, but now he's nought
Now I write this poem for him
It might be good or it might be dim
He's a:

    Person-creeper
    Fly-eater
    Web-maker
    Ceiling-taker
    Wall-header
    Eight-legger
    Quick-walker
    Non-talker
    Wall-climber
    Quick-timer
    Bed-explorer
    Cardboard-tourer.

Lauren Whelan (11)
Pooltown Community Junior School, Ellesmere Port

WAR

War is horrible
I can see blood stained everywhere
It's frightening when the sirens go off
I hate war
Because we shall never forget
Whose died or who is dying
It makes me feel like crying
Everyone must be dying
Guns go off around me
I don't like war
Because it's unforgettable when people die
In the end, we will be slaves for Germany
Because we will lose the war
I wish war would go away!

Richard Mason (10)
Pooltown Community Junior School, Ellesmere Port

MY CAT

My cat is called Mitzi
Sits where she was to sitzi
She sleeps all day and sleeps all night
And wakes up early and bright
She catches rats and catches mice
Eats them up, lovely and nice
But one day she ran away, very far
And got knocked over by a car
Now she's buried with a cross for a headstone
Now she's gone I'm all alone.

Katy Hughes (10)
Pooltown Community Junior School, Ellesmere Port

FISHING

When I go fishing I will catch a big fish,
two hours later I'd eat it on a dish.
Pike is a nasty fish and a fighter too,
it will eat my fish and maybe you.
A perch is coming to eat your bait,
you'd better catch him quickly before it's too late.
A roach is annoying so get him bad,
that's it, just like that lad.
A big fish like a carp is what you want,
it can be a different colour, maybe a font.
A bream is the smallest, colourful too
if you catch him he'd turn grey to blue.
A mackerel is white
and the best thing it does is fight.

Jack Bailey (11)
Pooltown Community Junior School, Ellesmere Port

AUTUMN

The autumn brings the howling wind,
The trees start to blush
As her dancing leaves drift off down the street,
The rain gurgles in the grid.

The autumn brings the furious rain
As it bangs on my windowpane,
The clouds change their colour to grey,
In the autumn the fog blinds me with a blindfold,
The autumn brings the howling wind.

Amy Archer (11)
Pooltown Community Junior School, Ellesmere Port

PERSONIFICATION

The dancing leaves fell off the trees,
The grass was breathing in the breeze.

The leaves are dancing like a ballet dancer,
The trees were acting like a prancer.

The man is sweeping the leaves with his mop,
The wind blows as the hailstones hop.

The lightning's running for the treetops,
The wind is hitting all the crops.

The leaves are talking to each other,
They are saying, 'I have a tree for a mother.'

Then the sun says goodbye
And all the grass gives a sigh.

Chris Ellery (11)
Pooltown Community Junior School, Ellesmere Port

MY MESSY BEDROOM

My messy bedroom is a total mess,
It can drive you up the wall sometimes it is a real pest,
My mum's always shouting, 'Get your room tidied.'
But I don't listen to a word she says.

My messy bedroom has lots of things you can tread on.
Oops, there goes my foot again,
With my messy bedroom is a total guarantee,
I want a new bedroom, please, please help me!

Michaela Drewery (11)
Pooltown Community Junior School, Ellesmere Port

WINTER POEM

In the winter it's snowy
It makes your nose glowy
We play in the snow
And Santa goes, 'Ho, ho.'

I make a snowman
With my friend Dan.
And all the leaves
Have gone from the trees.

We throw snowballs
And play on the ice and everyone falls.
Presents under the tree,
Open them and let's see.

Ben Clarke (11)
Pooltown Community Junior School, Ellesmere Port

AUTUMN'S HERE

It's getting cold and slightly chilly,
singing songs like Dilly and Dilly.

The air is cold, foggy too,
that's because the autumn's due.

The children giggle, they're wrapped up warm,
the mist slowly stalks them more and more.

The howling wind goes passing by,
the trees all gasp and say, 'My oh my!'

Rebecca Bills (10)
Pooltown Community Junior School, Ellesmere Port

WEATHER POEM

Mr Snowman was cold in winter,
he had caught an icicle splinter.
He got wrapped up with a scarf and hat,
but not for long, up jumped the cat.
Bit it off his cold, bald head,
made the snow on his body spread.
Now the snow is falling badly,
it's hitting the ground,
when you listen carefully you can hear
the happy sound.

Mr Snowman looks very cold,
if you build them high they look bold.
You wish you could put them in your house,
but they would just melt.
It's best to keep them in the street,
instead of freezing your cosy feet.

Mr Snowman turned very cold and froze,
he had an icicle on the end of his nose.
We need to keep him under a shelter,
because he even could just melt there.
We want to keep him as long as we can
then he'll be the longest lasting snowman.
So let's put him in the street,
and then he will just finally meet
a new snowman as a friend
that's my poem and that's the end.

Kimberley Jones (11)
Pooltown Community Junior School, Ellesmere Port

AN ENVIRONMENTAL POEM

Think about the food we eat,
some people eat fruit, some people eat meat.
I like to eat fruit and veg,
but all the best are round the edge.
I like my food the right colour and right shape,
and my favourite is a nice juicy grape.
Farmers keep their fruit nice and clean
and usually you can't grow a bean.

I always eat big red apples,
but most of all they're best in a chapel.
People don't like mud on carrots,
so they give them to the parrots.

Nicholas Gilmovitch (10)
Pooltown Community Junior School, Ellesmere Port

SCHOOL

School is where you learn
School is where you listen
School is where you concentrate
School is where you do maths and language
School is where we play games with our friends
School is where we all play together.

Isobel Woodhouse (7)
Richard Thornton's CE Primary School, Burton in Lonsdale

BONFIRE NIGHT

Rockets raising, rushing round and round
Bonfire blazing, burning bright
Bangers banging in the night
Sausages sizzling, standing on sticks
Silvery sparklers, shivering, shooting colourful sparks
Frightening fire, furious flames, fighting fools
Tons of tasty, terrific treacle toffee treats
Chattering children collecting conkers and playing catch
Gorgeous goodies, golden and good ginger
Naughty, noisy, noisy children having nothing to do.

Bang! Bang! Bash!

Eleanor Woodhouse (10)
Richard Thornton's CE Primary School, Burton in Lonsdale

MY NEW SCHOOL

My new school is so cool
and the headmaster is no fool
he can even play pool.

When we're in class we do English,
history and maths.
You can't be daft
or we'll get no laughs.

At the end of the day
we play, play, play
and some of us even say,
'Hooray!'

Sam Fisher (7)
Richard Thornton's CE Primary School, Burton in Lonsdale

GARETH

His hair is always spiky,
It's called the 4-4-2,
Everybody loves him,
Girls, especially you!

The boys in my class hate him,
But I know much too well!
Really they're just jealous
'Cause they use his Shockwaves gel.

He's best mates with Will Young,
They went down a winding road,
I'd shower them with hugs
And kisses by the load!

He is the reason I play piano,
He has a Grade 8, you know!
He probably plays piano on his tracks,
So really, you can't say no!

If you do not listen
To what his heart wants to say,
Believe me my friend,
You'll definitely regret the day!

He admires Elvis,
He sang 'Suspicious Minds',
I think he likes chocolate,
Lots of different kinds.

He took his family on holiday,
Miami, I think it was,
Now he lives in Kensington
And his flat is very posh 'cause

His name is Gareth Gates
And we love him!

Bethany Scott (10)
Rishton Methodist Primary School, Blackburn

MY DAD'S CAR WON'T START

Dad's car won't start,
It will not go,
He thinks it's the battery,
He does not know.

He's had it for years,
It's like an old friend,
But when it won't start,
It drives him round the bend.

The colour has faded,
The seats are torn,
It still won't start,
He thinks the engine is worn.

It still won't start,
I'm late for school,
But my dad still says
His car is still cool.

Leanne Gillett (11)
Rishton Methodist Primary School, Blackburn

FRUIT

Fruit is very good to eat,
Most of it is very sweet.

Apples and pears are sweet to taste,
Lemons are sour, 'Don't eat in haste.'

Bananas have thick, yellow skins,
You never see them sold in tins.

There are soft fruits we call berries,
I love to eat lots of cherries.

Everyone should eat some fruit,
But try not to get it on your suit.

Charlotte Achaski (11)
Rishton Methodist Primary School, Blackburn

AUTUMN

Just at the beginning of autumn
all I can hear is . . .
doors squeaking,
dogs barking,
kids running,
pins dropping,
cars rumbling,
glasses smashing,
people talking,
feet scraping,
trains pounding,
snakes hissing,
dogs growling,
sea roaring,
clocks ticking,
sun shining,
leaves blowing,
babies crying,
birds chirping,
people yelling,
balls bouncing,
rain trickling,
aeroplanes flying,
people walking.

Adam Fisher (10)
Rishton Methodist Primary School, Blackburn

MY SCHOOL

My school is the best,
Better than all the rest,
Rishton Methodist is the name,
We will put your school to shame.

Lots of teachers all are great,
My teacher is my mate,
Mrs Dunderdale is my teacher,
She is the best and you can't beat her.

Lauren Redfearn (10)
Rishton Methodist Primary School, Blackburn

BRAIN TEASER

What kind of ants
Tear down trees?

What type of ants
Roll in the mud
To take their ease?

What kind of ants
Flap their ears
In the breeze?

What kind of ants
Spell their names
With two 'e's?

Sssssssshhh!
Don't tell,
It's a tease!

Kirsty Devlin (10)
St Gregory's RC CP School, Bolton

BURGLAR BILL

Creeping stealthily through the dark night,
is Burglar Bill with his flashlight.
Feather-light slippers upon his feet,
so not a sound should hit the street.

Lock your windows, lock your hoose,
Burglar Bill is on the loose!

He's out to steal your hard-earned treasures,
to stop him we must take tough measures.
Bolt the door, set the alarm,
to keep your family safe from harm.

Lock your windows, lock your hoose,
Burglar Bill is on the loose!

He spots a window open just an inch,
that's all he needs to rob and pinch.
With leather gloves and crowbar ready,
his hands not shaky, very steady.

Lock your windows, lock your hoose,
Burglar Bill is on the loose!

Inside the house he looks around,
he fills his bag with valuables found.
As he turns outside to go,
a man shouts, 'Stop thief,
off to the police we go!'

No need to lock your windows,
no need to lock your hoose.
Burglar Bill won't be bothering you,
because he's no longer on the

Loose!

Laura Collins (10)
St Gregory's RC CP School, Bolton

THE BAD NIGHT

There was once a scruffy dog
called Bob,
Whose owner went out at night
just to rob.

He broke into cars,
with bent iron bars,
With one big smash,
he shattered the glass.

Then off to the store,
he jemmied the door,
Once inside,
he needed to hide.

As across the floor,
under the door,
he saw a light flashing,
'Oh no.'

'Who's there?' said a policeman
who was out on his beat,
'Okay, I'll surrender
'cause I'm not a big spender.

Might as well spend a night in a cell,
'cause I'm not going to spend it all.'
'Come on, where is it?'
'Okay, it's in the mall.'

Anthony Dunn (10)
St Gregory's RC CP School, Bolton

THE FOREST OF FEAR

Walking through the woods
In the midnight hour,
The trees begin to fall
To the wind's power.

Images cascade
And intertwine,
The woodland is wet
And the woodland is mine!

The voices are distant,
The whistling is close,
The call of the wild
Like the wild is supposed!

The girl comes near,
But then disappears,
She speaks in a voice
That you could not hear.

'I come not to live,
I come to save,
Run right now,
The danger is grave.'

The owl stays awake,
Its life is at stake,
The gunshot is heard
And down comes the bird!

Kirsty McCabe & Joe Walmsley (10)
St Gregory's RC CP School, Bolton

THE BERMUDA TRIANGLE

The Bermuda Triangle,
Whirling, swirling,
Rocking slowly,
Slowly it sticks its big, open mouth out and
Thrashes and trashes,
Until it gobbles up the ship.

Waiting, waiting,
As the next victim approaches,
Roaring and screaming,
Suddenly a huge bolt,
A bolt of lightning sinks the ship
And there go the distant cries.

Spinning, spinning,
Around and around,
Heading towards the last surviving ship,
Facing it,
Eyes locked and
Boom!

The Bermuda Triangle
Is the victor once again.
Will any ship or man
Ever be the same?

Adam Millett (10)
St Gregory's RC CP School, Bolton

THE FOG

The fog came to destroy the city
and cover the houses with frost.
It is clear to everyone
this city has been lost.

The fog has frozen everything,
all in one night.
When I rose up that morning,
I had a terrible fright.

Jack Smith (10)
St Gregory's RC CP School, Bolton

THE BLINDS BURGLAR

The wind was as light as a feather,
The moon was as bright as the sun,
The blinds burglar came running,
Running, running,
The blinds burglar came running to the next house of sin.

He went to his hideout in Dover,
Where he had a soda,
He kept the blinds in the cupboard behind,
Behind, behind,
He kept them in the cupboard behind where no one could find them.

He got a couple more,
Then he got to his hideout door,
He had a game of pool,
Then he looked so cool,
Cool, cool,
He looked so cool when he had a game of pool.

He went to a famous person's house,
Where he saw a tiny, tiddly mouse,
And he didn't mind getting caught with all the blinds,
Blinds, blinds,
He didn't mind getting caught with all the blinds,

Christopher Pottage (9)
St Gregory's RC CP School, Bolton

THE WIND

Rustling through the street,
making the trees swish to and fro,
making the window creak,
making the inn sign sway.

Running through the big, old house,
knocking over big pot jars,
knocking over water pots,
knocking over pens and books.

Blowing cheeks, making them frozen,
blowing people's hair into their mouths,
blowing fingers, to make gloves be worn,
blowing toes, so socks need to be put on.

Lydia Killas-Riding (10)
St Gregory's RC CP School, Bolton

FOG!

Fog whispers around,
Creeping about the house,
Wrapping it slowly in
A ghostly veil.
Sneaking through unseen
Gaps, it dims all colour,
Covers doors and windows
In its misty curtain.
Slowly, bit by bit,
It swallows its prey until the house is merged
Into greyness and invisible clouds.

Isobel Hinks (11)
St Gregory's RC CP School, Bolton

SEASONS

Seeping through the black hour,
Snow-white icicles,
Trickle down
Upon the golden alley.

Mysteriously the midnight shrivels
And buds open into the twinkling twilight,
Whistling the song of a bird,
And the sparkling dance of the moon.

Blazing all its surroundings,
Burning the deep swirl of the blinding red mist,
Burning the deep, grey shadow of the frozen virgin frost,
Cackling and gurgling as all life laughs and twitters.

One last breath all life will take,
Upon the orange, crunchy earth,
Before the midnight hour comes once again,
And dresses the world in its fresh, white cotton wool.

Róisín Shryane (11)
St Gregory's RC CP School, Bolton

SUN

The big fireball in the sky
Don't go near or you'll melt and die
I use it to get my tan
And laze all day if I can
But the thing I like best
Is sitting by the pool so that I can rest.

Kerrie Barrett (11)
St Gregory's RC CP School, Bolton

THE JEWEL THIEF

The woods are as black as the night,
So the three bears wanted a fright,
Snap, crackle, pop, go the twigs above,
But the bears don't mind because this is what they love.

The nasty wolf follows his nose,
He finds a house then in he goes,
To his surprise a shining light
Takes him to the stone so bright.

He speeds to the jewel as fast as a car,
He can't help himself, that's how wolves are,
He grabs the jewel without much thought,
Like a mouse in a trap he is caught.

The tired bears come in at last,
Dying for a hot bath,
What do you think the bears see?
The wolf is trapped on the floor.

The jewel is safe, thank God for that,
So they ring the police to take the wolf back,
The bears are safe in the small cottage at last,
So they all take a big, hot, bubbly bath.

Jennifer Kavanagh (9)
St Gregory's RC CP School, Bolton

THE FOG

Around the creepy castle shrouding through the foggy mist,
gliding round the deep and dark moat.

An unknown creature's skeleton looking alive in the misty mist.
No one dared to even look at the creepy castle on top of the hill.

The howling of the wind shook the loose, stained glass windows
and whistled through the treetops.

The fog hung around the castle
like a white veil on its wedding day.

Rebecca Kendal (11)
St Gregory's RC CP School, Bolton

HONEY MONEY

There was once a girl named
Honey,
Who desperately wanted some
Money.

She went to a bank
But her heart went and sank,
When the bank said they had
No money.

The girl was in despair
So she sold her long hair
For a few pounds,
To get some money.

When that did not last
She thought about her past,
Which filled her with fear.
Oh! Poor little Honey.

To steal was her choice
And the crime had no voice,
And to prison went
Poor little Honey!

Bethany Reid (9)
St Gregory's RC CP School, Bolton

THE SUN

The sun shines down,
With its sizzling glare.
The sun is just too hot
To bear.

The sun is made of
Very hot gases,
Which will burn down
All of your glasses.

The sun shines down,
At nightfall,
As they all avoid the
Very bright ball.

Stephen Gaffney (11)
St Gregory's RC CP School, Bolton

WINTER'S TIMES

W indy breezes, scattered leaves everywhere leaving not even a
single patch of grass.
I n and out of every gap, ice blew its cold breath,
turning land into glass.
N ever had the snow made the ground so pearly white.
T ogether each of them soared through the night.
E ven the rain joined in to play.
R oaring around whilst bare trees shivered, they had to put up with it
for more than one day.

Alison Stones (10)
St Gregory's RC CP School, Bolton

THE PRINCESS DIAMOND

'Princess, Princess, what is your diamond?'
'Gold with a crystal, Goblin, why do you stare at it?'
'Give me it,'
'No.'
Give me it, give me it.

Then I will howl all night in the woods,
Run round leaves and fallen trees.'
'Goblin, why do you want the diamond so?'

'The crystals shine like stars.
I want to feel the roughness of the diamond,
The gold is like the shining sun.'

'Hush, I stole it from a hole in the ground.'
'Give me it.'
'No.'
'Give me it.'
'No.'
'Give me it.'
'No, why should I give it to you?'

'I need the diamond,'
'Why do you need it?'
'I need to give it to the queen goblin.'
'What will you give me?'

'I will give you anything.'
'Fine, you can have the diamond for a handsome prince.'
'Here's a handsome prince.'
So she gave him the diamond.

Stacey Gaffney (10)
St Gregory's RC CP School, Bolton

THE MAGIC BOX

One box of silver,
One box of gold,
One box of young,
One box of old.

What will we find in this box?
Who knows?

Some say a rabbit,
A hare or a fox.
Some say a bird
Is inside this box.

Is it an owl
Of all the night?
Or is it a parrot,
So colourful and bright?

It remains a secret,
What is inside.
Whatever it is
Still likes to hide.

Alex Alker (10)
St Gregory's RC CP School, Bolton

GOD'S CREATION

Lord thank you for mountains, full of joy.
Lord thank you for lakes and rivers full of glimmering water.
Lord thank you for the cold snow and the frost.
Lord thank you for the smell of flowers.

Frazer Leigh (8)
St Gregory's RC CP School, Bolton

HAIL

Drops of crystal falling from the sky
powerful and fast,
like bombs, all sizes,
different day,
whatever time
nesting in the gutter,
sticking to my shoe
and tapping on the window sill.
Christmas colour,
dashing down,
hitting my head
and
making
it hurt.

Nichola Nelson (10)
St Gregory's RC CP School, Bolton

THE FOG

Cloudy fog swam across me,
The thickness crept around the streets,
Wrapped around the slimy bog,
Sneered back at the lonely dog,
Growled to see the fabulous frog,
Gave a wink at the dirty log.
From all of this he isn't too friendly
Especially to his enemies, the sun and the ice,
Who are always following close behind.

Vicki Jones (11)
St Gregory's RC CP School, Bolton

SNOW

Falling fast, falling slow,
It starts high then finishes low,
Falling slow, falling fast,
It lies thick whilst days pass.

Round swirling, round whirling,
Very pretty, white and curling,
Swirling round, whirling round,
Then swiftly falling to the ground.

Spreading chills across the land,
Snowball fights are what kids demand,
Across the land chills are spreading,
Which makes the land like the gown of a wedding.
Everybody sees the grass all white,
Jack Frost has been in the night.
It makes me happy,
No one can say no,
That this is a great day,
Because we have . . .
    Snow.

Gabriella Magari (11)
St Gregory's RC CP School, Bolton

JESUS THE LORD

Jesus, when I see the mountains
I feel the power of your love.
Jesus, when I see the beautiful, fluffy snow
I feel the kindness of other people.
Jesus, when I see the flowing, rushing rivers
I feel the gentleness of you.

Elizabeth Laura Whittaker (9)
St Gregory's RC CP School, Bolton

THE FOG

The thick fog trailed over the grass
Destroying everything in its path.
It sneered back at what it had done
And thought it was great fun.

The thick fog trailed over the grass
Laughing at the mess on the ground.
It looked on the floor and looked in the air
And thought it was very bare.

The thick fog trailed over the grass
Making itself look very fast.
It looked at the trees and looked at the leaves
And frowned at the midnight breeze.

The thick fog trailed over the grass
Now it was very sad.
It couldn't destroy anything else
Because it had all disappeared.

So it trailed away to its home.

Abbi Sargent (10)
St Gregory's RC CP School, Bolton

THE DARK

The dark is as black as night
The dark gives me a fright
The dark gives babies the creeps
The dark makes old people peep
The dark is as black as the haunted house.
The dark scares me!

Katie Litherland (8)
St Gregory's RC CP School, Bolton

SNOW

Snow is cold and icy,
Snow lands on high hills
And colourful mountain tops.

Snow is a silent sound,
You can't hear a thing
When snow drops.

Snow grips on walls
and sticks on window
ledges and doors.

The snow sprinkles
Itself around the house
and in the garden.

Tayler Booker (11)
St Gregory's RC CP School, Bolton

LOVE

When I saw the mountains and the beautiful rivers,
it amazed me.
I saw the wonderful lake which was dark blue
and it was wonderful.
I've seen the lovely snow, shining
on the mountain tops.
I can see and smell the flowers which bloom
in my lovely garden.
I love all of these things in winter,
summer, fall or spring.

Amen

Michelle Jansen (9)
St Gregory's RC CP School, Bolton

HAIL

Slipping down the street
Hailstones crackled and bounced
And tapping on the windows
Startled the dog.

Sliming and blinding, the
Hailstones built up on the car
Windscreen.

Petrifying and loud, the
Hailstones rattled and tapped
With their icy, thin fingers.

Binding together and frozen,
The hailstones fell on the floor and grazed their knees.

The simpering, slimy stones
Swivelled down the street all the time
And griped their hands on the pathways.

Louise Rushton (10)
St Gregory's RC CP School, Bolton

WHEN I LOOK

Lord, when I look at mountains
I think of people climbing up
and falling down.
Lord, when I look at lakes and rivers
it reminds me of people drowning,
but your hand will save them.
Lord, when I look at clear, white snow
I know that you are with me.

Rachel Booth (8)
St Gregory's RC CP School, Bolton

GOD'S WONDERFUL WORLD

Thank you God for the flowers that grow
in summer and die in winter,
they give us a fresh feeling.
Thank you God for the high
mountains which soar through
the clear, blue sky.
When I see snow, it makes me think
of a sick person whom you will soon save.
I see fast flowing rivers which rush
and push through the hard stones.

Alix Whitelaw (8)
St Gregory's RC CP School, Bolton

PLAYING FOOTBALL

Crowds cheering
Elderly jeering
Mud splattering
Mothers chattering
Balls bouncing
Players pouncing
Free kicks bending
Matches ending.

Kieran Almond (9)
St Gregory's RC CP School, Bolton

SUN

Stretching and yawning,
I raise my head,
Warm arms unfold
To get you out of bed.

Feel my rays
Sent to warm you through,
Sit in a chair and
Laze the whole day through.

Hannah Rose Moss (10)
St Gregory's RC CP School, Bolton

IN THE NIGHT

Wolves howling
 Cats meowing
  Broomsticks flying
   People crying
    Spiders spinning
     Witches winning
      Vampires sucking
       People looking.

Rosie Nelson (8)
St Gregory's RC CP School, Bolton

YOUR WORLD

Lord, when I see the mountains
I feel the power of your hands.
Lord, when I see lakes I feel
the stillness of your world.
Snow, snow is so soft,
like a newborn baby.
Lord, when I see the flowers
I see the strength of your heart.

Amen

Scott Woodcock (9)
St Gregory's RC CP School, Bolton

COLOURS

If I had wings
I would touch the stars, shining brightly
in the midnight sky.
If I had wings
I would taste the cheese of the moon
as I fly by.
If I had wings,
I would gaze in amazement at the
loving angels in the wispy, summer sky.
If I had wings,
I would listen to the soft, gentle singing
of the kind, loving angel up in Heaven.
If I had wings,
I would hear the colourful birds singing
in the cold, winter sky.
If I had wings,
I would dream of wonderful, green fields
and grape trees rushing by, as wispy clouds
push me across the clear blue sky.

Charlotte Killas-Riding (9)
St Gregory's RC CP School, Bolton

SCHOOL

School is a magical place,
Where strange things happen.
Where teachers can turn into deadly monsters
And children can turn into whatever they want.
Where maths and literacy don't exist
And where fun, fun and more fun exist.
Where words leap out of pages and dance around.

Liam Priestley (11)
St Gregory's RC CP School, Bolton

THE UNDERWEAR ROBBERS

This woman once did shoplift
She shoplifted from Next,
But what she did not know was they had got
Stuck to her leg - so
She shoved it in her shoe but it popped out
Near her toe, so
She got embarrassed then, so she walked
out the door.

Next, she sent her best friend,
But she forgot her bag,
She didn't know what to do,
So she phoned up her Dad,
She tied the underwear to her legs,
To her father she just said they were pegs.

When the police found out where they lived,
They styled their hair like men.
When the police arrived,
They sat at their desk
All stuffed with underwear like fat, fat men
One had a pen
And one was in her den.

The police asked them to go down town,
When they walked out the door,
Their underwear fell down.
Just then they were arrested, with
A big, big frown.

In the police cell
One said we're in Hell.
The other one was laughing with joy,
For her dad had come for her.

Danielle Potter (9)
St Gregory's RC CP School, Bolton

FOG

Shhh, shhh, off it goes.
Is it fog, no one knows?
Well then, let's wait and see
Until we can't see our frozen nose.

Layla Bradley (10)
St Gregory's RC CP School, Bolton

THE SEA IS . . .

The sea is a playful dolphin
Grey and blue.
Shining and reflecting
All night through.
Twirling, splashing
Against the rocks,
Singing and dancing
With the ships,
Gliding and jumping
For all to see.

Rebecca Carroll (10)
St Mary's RC Primary School, Langho

THE SEA IS A CAT

The sea is a cat,
Leaping up and down,
Playing all day long and sleeping in the night,
Glinting in bright sunlight,
Sweeping up anything in its path
Because of its impatient wrath.

Joe Peplow (9)
St Mary's RC Primary School, Langho

THAT TERRIBLE FEELING

That terrible feeling,
Your stomach thumps,
You hear the footsteps,
Like a sound of booming jumps.

The footsteps come nearer,
Your heart burns in fear,
But you're stuck in the trap,
All hope disappears.

The fires of Hell
Rage and sizzle inside,
You see what you dread,
To start a frightful ride.

If flames were to be words,
The rooms would be burnt,
After the shoutin' he's given me,
To be bad I daren't.

Fergal Kinney (9)
St Mary's RC Primary School, Langho

THE ANIMALS INSIDE ME

There is a shark inside me that makes me king of the water,
There is a bear inside me that will be angry, tossing things everywhere,
There is a panda inside me that makes me very, very lazy,
There is a polar bear inside me that makes me like cold weather
and snow,
There is a bushbaby inside me that makes me wide awake,
There is a gorilla inside me that makes me a gentle giant.

George Barnes (9)
St Mary's RC Primary School, Langho

MY BEST FRIEND, HELEN

My best friend, Helen,
I don't know what I'd do,
If she went to another school.
I'd probably think it's coz of me,
Was I acting like a fool?

My best friend, Helen,
I don't know what to say.
She has a twin called Jane,
To tell the truth, I don't think
They look at all the same.

My best friend, Helen,
She rings me every day,
She tells me to wrap up warm,
She does the weather forecast,
In a very silly way.

That's the way she's made!

Emily Clarkson (10)
St Mary's RC Primary School, Langho

KITTENS, CATS AND MITTENS

Furry and cute are cats,
Sweet and soft are kittens,
But if they're cute or if they're sweet,
They like to rip up mittens.

They will rip up mittens every day,
With their tails, heads or paws,
Cotton hanging from their mouths,
Thread swaying from their claws.

Nicola Cloney (9)
St Mary's RC Primary School, Langho

WATER

The Lord put fish in the water,
The Lord put fish in the sea,
If we did not pollute water,
Think how many fish there would be!

The Lord made the world just for us,
He wanted us all to be free,
But if we shared our food with others,
Think how fair we would be!

If we all tried together,
And didn't drop things in the sea,
If we did not pollute the air,
Think how happy the Lord would be!

Dominic Hartley (9)
St Mary's RC Primary School, Langho

THERE'RE ANIMALS INSIDE ME

There is a dolphin inside me which jumps
and swims very softly.
There is a polar bear inside me which plays
in the frosty snow.
There is a dog inside me which runs
and plays in the windy fields.
There is a kangaroo inside me which plays
in the deserts.
There is a cat inside me which climbs
up trees with its claws.
There is a cheetah inside me which runs,
chasing for its prey.

Johanna Coyne (10)
St Mary's RC Primary School, Langho

MINK AND RAT

'My teeth are sharp and white, Rat,'
'I see them sparkling now, Mink.'
'I'll catch you easily now, Rat,
'I'll run away from you, Mink.'
'Where can you hide from me, Rat?'
'Down my little drain, Mink.'
'I'll be faster than you, Rat,'
'I'll start running, now, Mink.'
'My paws are soft and padded, Rat,'
'I'll always hear you coming, Mink.'
'I'll swipe out at you now, Rat,'
'Ha, you missed again, Mink.'
'You'll never get away, Rat,'
'I can see the drain, Mink.'
'I will catch you first, Rat,'
'I'll jump down the drain, Mink.'
'Where did you go, Rat?'
'I am down my drain, Mink.'
'My teeth are sharp and white, Rat.'

James Golding (9)
St Mary's RC Primary School, Langho

THE ANIMALS INSIDE ME

There is a cat inside me which rolls up in a ball in winter and
                                                    keeps itself warm.
There is a parrot inside me which talks and talks too much.
There is a shark inside me which can swim very well.
There is an elephant inside me which gets me mad and very angry.
There is a kangaroo inside me which is very excited and jumpy.

Francesca Bellanca (9)
St Mary's RC Primary School, Langho

THE RAINFOREST

Tigers prowling,
Lions roaring,
Wagging and yawning.

Parrots squawking,
Frogs jumping, burping,
Snakes hissing.

Toucans talking,
Talking loudly,
Talking softly.

Cheetah running, eating,
Giraffe stretching
His long neck.

Fish swimming,
Swimming fast,
Swimming slow.

Niamh McCarthy (10)
St Mary's RC Primary School, Langho

I LIKE TO PLAY SPORT

I like to play football, I like to play sport,
I like to play tennis on the big, green court.

I like to play cricket,
I always hit the wicket.

I like to do running
Because it's so cunning.

Lewis Cassidy (10)
St Mary's RC Primary School, Langho

IRISH DANCING

I rish dancing is my hobby,
R iverdance is like the same,
I love dancing, it's such fun,
S arah can do a little dance,
H opping, skipping, I like that.

D resses are designed fab,
A nna, my sister, can do a dance,
N iamh, my dancing friend, is good.
C razy Rebecca is good as well,
I know about 7 or 8 dances,
N o it's fantastic,
G oing there at 10am.

Beth Jameson (9)
St Mary's RC Primary School, Langho

THE SEA IS . . .

The sea is a wolf,
rushing about splashing,
determined to catch its prey,
jumping and crashing
through the night.
At night it howls
as the waves crash.
In the day the sun shines
and its eyes sparkle
in the sunlight.
In winter it will rest
ready for the next summer.

Bethany Thompson (9)
St Mary's RC Primary School, Langho

FOREST FIRE!

Crying! Crying!
Stress is running through my mind.
Crying! Crying!
Can't stop running through the fire.

Must escape the burning fire,
Must escape the mighty blazes,
Red, yellow, orange, green and amber.

Chaos! Chaos!
There's destruction in our habitat,
Our houses are on fire,
We can't escape the mighty fire,
    Forest fire.

Jordan Brooks (10)
St Mary's RC Primary School, Langho

SNAKE

Hiss, hiss,
Stop staring
With your brown eyes!
How tall you are,
But I could still
Swallow you whole!
I slither slowly across the rock.
Stop looking through the glass!
I say,
'Why don't you join me for lunch?'
My body shines and whispers-s-s.

Sam Rushton (8)
St Mary's RC Primary School, Langho

THE LUCKY LOTTO TICKET

There I was in my shop,
In a strop,
My workers were bad,
I was so mad.

The children were throwing candy,
I needed a brandy,
I was in a stress,
The shop was a mess.

I bought myself a Lotto ticket,
Then left and saw my husband playing cricket,
We went back home,
He'd broken a bone!

We watched the tele,
With our daughter, Kelly,
On the lottery we had found,
We had just won £66,000,000!

Jane Keegan (10)
St Mary's RC Primary School, Langho

SNAKE

Slimy, slithery snake
Hisses along the ground
Searching for its prey.
Snakes will search for anything,
They might even search for you!
So if you ever hear a hissing sound,
Just stay still and be . . . calm.

Jack Blackwell (9)
St Mary's RC Primary School, Langho

THE DRAGON AND THE GORILLA

'Hello, how are you feeling today, Gorilla?'
'Who me? I'm perfectly fine, Dragon.'
'If you are you won't be soon, Gorilla.'
'I'm getting away, Dragon.'
'No you are not, Gorilla.'
'I'm just as fast as you , Dragon.'
'How do you know, Gorilla?'
'I know because I'm on your back, Dragon!'
'I can't feel anything, Gorilla.'
'You should now, Dragon.'
'Don't hit me on the head, Gorilla.'
'Why shouldn't I, Dragon?'
'I give up, Gorilla.'
'That's what I wanted to hear, Dragon.'

Christopher Darbyshire (8)
St Mary's RC Primary School, Langho

MY GRAN'S PLUMP CAT

Whenever I go to my gran's,
Her cat's always on her knee.
My gran thinks she's grand,
But I think it's a big fat flea.

Whenever I go to my gran's,
Her cat's always on her knee.
I'm never going there for tea
And guess what?
My gran's plump, purple cat,
Is about thirty-three.

Gina Croston (10)
St Mary's RC Primary School, Langho

THE STAR AND THE SUN

'Why do you shine in the day, Sun?'
'Why do you shine at night, Star?'
'You are very wrong, Sun.'
'I am very right, Star.'
'You can be too hot, Sun.'
'No one sees your light, Star.'
'What's the point of you, Sun?'
'Why do you bother, Star?'
'Why do you shine in the day, Sun?'
'Why do you shine at night, Star?'
'You are very wrong, Sun.'
'I am very right, Star.'

Brigid O'Reilly (8)
St Mary's RC Primary School, Langho

HELL

The fires of Hell,
There's no time for a funeral bell,
The burning red,
As people in bed
Can hear the screaming
As fire's beaming
Lava rises,
Brings bad surprises.
The rocks start to fall,
Bringing a call,
The demon has awoken,
As legends have spoken.

Michael James Mooney (10)
St Mary's RC Primary School, Langho

THE SUN

The summer sun is burning like a cigarette
In the cloudless blue sky,
Cooking people alive.

The summer is like burning hot sand
In the cloudless blue sky,
Burning people's feet.

The summer sun is like a ball of fire
In the cloudless blue sky,
Turning my skin into leather.

The winter sun is like a dim light
In the cloudy grey sky,
Freezing people alive.

Francis Baker (11)
St Mary's RC Primary School, Langho

THE GOAL BY ANDY COLE

What a goal by Andy Cole,
In the final, what a dream.
All the Blackburn Rovers fans laugh and shout
About that glorious, happy day.
All the Spurs fans groan and cry,
He came from Manchester United.
What a deal, he is a natural goal machine
And now we have Dwight Yorke,
The rest of The Premiership watch out,
Forget the Champions League or the FA Cup,
Andy Cole scored the goal to make it 2-1 in the Worthington Cup Final.

Joe McCreadie (11)
St Mary's RC Primary School, Langho

THE BUBBLEGUM PARTY

Nutty tart,
Football crazy,
Dancing queen,
Boy racer.

Slap head,
Disco diva,
Groovy chick,
Diamond geezer.

Ginger nut,
Beer belly,
Sofa spud,
Always watching the telly.

Fitness freak,
Cutie pie,
Honey bunny
Who's always shy.

This is the bubblegum party,
Sorry not all of them could come,
But I'm sure that they're
all having fun.

Rachael Manning & Emily Hurst (11)
St Mary's RC Primary School, Langho

PANDAS

Pandas with big, black paws,
Black and white bodies,
The panda's hand clutches
A bamboo stick.
His big eyes look like they are sad.

Who is that human,
So small,
So far away?
What are they doing?
What's that flash?

Imogen McCreadie (8)
St Mary's RC Primary School, Langho

CHOOSING CHOCOLATE

Walking to Spar,
For my chocolate bar,
My mouth is watering
As I enter the store.
I stand in the aisle,
Looking at the lovely lot,
I can't decide.
Is it time for a Dime
Or should I click for a Twix?
Gazing at the creamy Dream,
I can't decide.
Maybe a chocolate with gooey caramel inside
Or an Aero with bubbles that make trouble.
Oh! The wrappers, the beautiful blues,
The glittering golds,
The shiny silvers,
The cherry-red wrappers.
I reach for the chosen one,
Pay for my piece of paradise
And walk outside
To crack the snap of my chocolate bar.

Peter Kellaway (11)
St Mary's RC Primary School, Langho

CYCLOPS

Cyclops is funnier than a joker,
Slimmer than a piece of paper,
Angrier than the world's strongest man,
Taller than a skyscraper,
Fatter than the world's fattest turkey,
Hairier than a gorilla,
And heavier than the *Earth.*

Sam Walsh (8)
St Mary's RC Primary School, Langho

MY DOG, PIPPA

My dog, Pippa runs all around,
She jumps on the sofa and lies down!
She runs in the sea and chases ducks,
But the current's too strong for her and she has bad luck.

We take her for a walk nearly every day,
She gets off her lead and runs away!
She tries catching rabbits and misses everyone,
She comes back at last and lies in front of the fire.

Shaun Ward (10)
St Mary's RC Primary School, Langho

THE FOREST FIRE!

Scurry! Scurry!
Running away from the blazing fire.
Scurry! Scurry!
Must run away from the falling trees.

Terror! Terror!
All the animals run and hide.
Terror! Terror!
All the floor is covered in ash!

Michael Clegg (10)
St Mary's RC Primary School, Langho

SLITHERY SNAKE

Snake slithers over the ground,
He hisses with his sound,
He wraps himself around a tree,
He senses with his tongue.
His skin is shiny like a golden ribbon,
He rubs against logs to shed his skin.
Snakes poison with their venomous fangs.

Rory Mansfield (8)
St Mary's RC Primary School, Langho

SUN AND CLOUD

'You cannot win now, Cloud.'
'I think I can, Sun.'
'I am already shining, Cloud.'
'So what if you're shining, Sun.'
'Now, don't spoil the day, Cloud.'
'But I want to rain, Sun.'
'Well, I am sorry, you can't, Cloud.'
'The people need rain to live, Sun.'

Megan Meredith (9)
St Mary's RC Primary School, Langho

My Best Friend

My best friend, Emily C,
She makes me laugh so easily,
Her piano smile is very long,
Wanting to be a kick-boxer, she must be very strong.

Her family are all crazy,
The only thing she's not is lazy,
She can get up at seven,
But never at eleven.

I've known her since I was four
And she'll never bore.
She's totally in trend
And she's my special friend.

Helen Keegan (10)
St Mary's RC Primary School, Langho

My Dog, Jazz

I have a dog called Jazz,
I take him out for walks,
I take him to the park
and barking's how he talks.

My dog, Jazz, is like David Beckham,
because he is great at football,
My dog, Jazz can head it too
despite being small.

I love my dog, Jazz
because he is great,
for he is very special to me
and he is my best mate.

Elle Vernon (11)
St Mary's RC Primary School, Langho

THERE WAS A MAN CALLED AUSTIN

There was a man called Austin Powers,
He had big teeth and wore suits with flowers.
Doctor Evil and Mini Me
Were the ultimate enemy,
'Groovy baby,' was what he said,
He chased girls and had street cred:
Doctor Evil had him on the run
But Austin Powers always won!

Catherine Darbyshire (10)
St Mary's RC Primary School, Langho

THERE WAS A COPPER CALLED PETE

There was a copper called Pete
Who had awfully malodorous feet,
His colleagues said, 'Pooh!
What on earth's in that shoe?
You smell like an old piece of meat!'

Thomas Broome (10)
St Mary's RC Primary School, Langho

THE LION AND THE SOLDIER

'I am very hungry, Soldier.'
'Don't look at me, Lion.'
'Now for my dessert, Soldier,'
'You're not eating me, Lion.'
'Oh yes I am, Soldier.'
'Only if you catch me, Lion.'
'1, 2, 3, ready or not, here I come, Soldier.'
'I'm too fast for you, Lion.'

Alex Mullin (8)
St Mary's RC Primary School, Langho

THE RIVER'S JOURNEY

I am a sparkling, gushing river rich with trout and salmon,
gurgling and laughing in my beautiful, clear water.
I swiftly slide along my path
and then the rapids take a hand
and violently speed towards meadows of sheep and cows.
I rush down valleys of fresh morning dew on the fresh grass
and then I take a moment to glisten in the marvellous sunshine.
I tumble down a waterfall
while trickles of water flicker in the air.
I switch ever so slowly and enter the forest
where I meet my friend, the deer,
he comes to drink from my lovely, sweet water.
Now I swim towards a glimpse of light at the end of the tropical forest
and feel the warmth of the sun.
I swim across my path and fall down a waterfall
where I finally shatter into droplets of crystal-clear water.

I turn towards the kingfisher who stands on a rock in the heart of me,
now I flick my drips to the side as I come across the heron,
who pinches my trout and drinks from my cool, sparkling water.
This is the place where I belong,
a place of harmony,
but this won't last for ever
for now I am swimming into a field with cattle and, without notice,
I approach a huge, dismal, dark shadow of a pollution monster.
He takes me inside, so I rage furiously.
My rapids get restless and start to be violent
and speed towards the wall of the monstrous thing.
My rapids fail and I get taken into the humungous giant,
full of gas and lots of fumes and diesel.
Oil and petrol squirt down on me
and chemicals hurl and vomit towards me
as if you were standing under a waterfall and it spat on you.

My fresh water is turning into a muddy pool of filth,
this is my worst nightmare ever and probably my last.
I weep in sorrow and try to make my shrill cry be heard,
so I start to shriek to shoot out my darkest fear,
the chemicals within my filthy surface,
but wait, I see a light of hope,
a twinkle of joy for now I can see me coming to life again,
a pipe of clean water comes out from my water's edge
and, when I think it is all over, civilisation sees me
stranded on my deathbed and decides to help.
This is the story of my life!
Now I am back to a flume just like the old days!

Curtis Booth (10)
St Mary's RC Primary School, Langho

MY MUM

My mum's caring no matter what I say,
My mum loves me in every single way,
I love her too,
No matter what people say,
Because she is my mum!

My mum's patient when I am busy,
My mum listens to me when I am sad,
My mum is my second best friend.
If something happened to her,
I wouldn't know what to do
Because I love my mum.

Amy Scholes (10)
St Mary's RC Primary School, Langho

MY DOG, SUGAR

My dog, Sugar
    Is black and white,
        She has small paws,
            But she can fight!

My dog, Sugar
    Has a nice blue eye,
        She is quite small
            But in a way she acts quite tall.

My dog, Sugar,
    She is a tugger,
        She likes to play tennis with a big, green ball
            But sometimes she gets in a fight with my other dog, Spice.

My dog, Sugar,
    She is quite noisy,
        But who cares?
            She's my Sugar!

Emma Hill (10)
St Mary's RC Primary School, Sabden

WITCH'S POTION

10 things found in a witch's potion . . .

Newts' heads
and spiders' legs.
Frogs' toes
and a slug's nose.
Cows' horns
and poison bushes' thorns.

Girls' eyes
and big brown pies.
Rosie's hair
and a little chair.

That's what I would put in my potion, *bang!*

Alex Reid (9)
St Mary's RC Primary School, Sabden

THE MYSTERY THING

He glides through the night,
as silently as can be.
He goes into houses to check the children are asleep

The mysterious thing's coming
tonight, tonight.

He has a lantern with a flame
as dim as he,
A black swishing cloak the colour of
the night sky,
A black cloth hides his mysterious face.

The mysterious thing's coming
tonight, tonight.

He holds an axe,
as shiny as a firework bursting into stars.
No one sees this fantasy thing.

The mysterious thing's coming
tonight, tonight.

Kathryn Clarkson (9)
St Mary's RC Primary School, Sabden

EASTER

Easter is the time of year,
Not Christmas or New Year.
Yet a sense of holiness is in the air.
Chocolate is spread like a blanket,
Easter is here, let's give a big cheer!

Emma Bromley (10)
St Mary's RC Primary School, Sabden

SCHOOL DINNERS

School dinners are disgusting,
I'm going to make a complaint,
Each day when I'm in the dinner queue,
I very nearly faint.

With soggy chips and burgers
And sunken Yorkshire puds
Accompanied by cremated meatballs
And poisoned boiled spuds.

I bite into a meatball
Really spicy hot
I'll maybe take another bite
On the other hand, maybe not.

I started choking badly
My eyeballs started flooding
And if you're thinking that's the lot
Don't let me start on pudding!

Rosie O'Gorman (10)
St Mary's RC Primary School, Bacup

WHEN GOOFY GOOFBALL CAME TO TOWN

When Goofy Goofball came to town,
He came in the goofiest spaceship I know.
It was yellow and blue
And stuck with glue,
Oh, he was the goofiest goofball of all.
I went inside and what a sight,
All inside was whitewash white,
Oh, he was the goofiest goofball of all.
We had some globs and grease,
Plus all the plates were creased,
Oh, he was the goofiest goofball of all.
When it was time to go home,
He gave me a little gnome
To remember the goofiest goofball of all.

Melanie Batt (11)
St Mary's RC Primary School, Bacup

LONELINESS

L   oneliness is grey,
O   n your own all day,
N   ever-ending emptiness,
E   verlasting loneliness,
L   ying on your bed,
I   nside, you want some friends instead,
N   obody cares about you,
E   very day you're feeling blue,
S   omebody's come to cheer you up with a
S   teaming mug of hot chocolate, in a cup.

Jade Marsden (10)
St Mary's RC Primary School, Bacup

THE BESTEST DAD IN THE WORLD

The bestest dad in the world has to be mine.
If I ask for some money he says, 'Yes, that's fine.'
He lets me buy a chocolate Flake
And he must be stronger than an earthquake.
He takes me to McDonald's like a shooting star
And he takes me in his super-fast car.
This is the end of this poem,
But at night there's only one star showing.

Lauren Watton (8)
St Mary's RC Primary School, Bacup

THE BIG MONSTER

It's the big monster, all will be scared,
Don't try and catch it, no one has ever dared.
It's the big monster, let's all shout,
Or get a big bat and give it a clout.
It's the big monster, don't try and kill it,
Just get a slingshot and that'll thrill it.
You killed the big monster, it is dead,
You got a gun and shot it in the head!

Ryan O'Connor (8)
St Mary's RC Primary School, Bacup

HAPPINESS

Some people spread happiness
Wherever they go
If they don't, believe me
It will show.

At my school we all spread happiness
We all shine like the sun
We all like one another
We aren't nasty to anyone.

Shannon Connolly (10)
St Mary's RC Primary School, Bacup

THE LITTLE FOX

The little fox met as he was walking
A piggy who never stopped talking.
He laughed and he giggled,
He stuttered and wiggled,
And gave little jumps and jiggled.

The fox said to Piggy, 'Shut up!'
'Oh I will,' said Piggy.
'Here take a cup,
Come into my house
And have some woodlouse,
And come and meet my pet mouse.'

The fox said, 'Charmed, I'm sure.
I suppose it will really cure
The headache I've had,
It's really quite bad
And would really make me very glad.'

So the fox marched into his house
And he met on the doorstep a mouse,
It screeched with great fear,
It went right through his ear,
And he was deaf for nearly a year.

Catherine Hampson (11)
St Mary's RC Primary School, Bacup

BIRTHDAYS

Every time on my birthday
I shout, 'It's today!' with glee.
I say, 'Hooray, hooray, hooray!'
Yes, it's my birthday for me.

People come in and sit down
Singing 'Happy Birthday' to me.
Auntie gave me a silk dressing gown
I asked them to stay for tea.

When I've opened my things
I want more and more.
Then my grandma brings
My new bedroom door.

When the day is nearly done
I wish it could stay forever.
The candles on the birthday cake shone
My sister was under the weather.

Helen Anderson (9)
St Oswald's Knuzden CE Primary School, Blackburn

MY FAVE TEDDIES

My teddies talk to me
They are very noisy
When I tell them to shut up
They say I am so crazy
My unicorn is furry
It looks a bit scary
Harvey is the best teddy in the world.

Anna Walsh (9)
St Oswald's Knuzden CE Primary School, Blackburn

BLACKPOOL

Roller coaster, Ferris wheel, dodgems,
Millions of people
Eating
Playing
Screaming
Laughing
Crying
Shaking
Dripping
Lining up for the roller coaster
Down hills
Round loops
Through tunnels
Upside down
Really fast and scary
People who come off are soaking man, soaking!

Jonathan Whittam (9)
St Oswald's Knuzden CE Primary School, Blackburn

ASK PUPPY

I went to ask Mummy but
Mummy said, 'Ask Daddy.'
I went to ask Daddy and
Daddy said, 'Go away.'
So I went to ask puppy.
Puppy always says yes.
Puppy comes everywhere with me,
Except the swimming pool.

Jessica Baldwin (8)
St Oswald's Knuzden CE Primary School, Blackburn

MONTSERRAT

Holidays and sunny days,
You see we're going to Montserrat for our holidays.
I can't wait to see the sunny days
And eat my coconut.

My ears go ping,
I don't know what to sing.
I'm going to my homeland, I go ding,
Montserrat is my favourite place.

When people say my name,
It's just a shame.
I'm being a pain.
Montserrat is the greatest place I've ever lived.

Arianne Piper (9)
St Oswald's Knuzden CE Primary School, Blackburn

THE FISH

The fish was playing around
Flipping his tail
He was happy.
A tomcat came to the window
Thinking of a plan.
He was hungry
The cat was thin
He went behind the fish bowl
And hit it with his paw.
It wobbled, it wobbled more
More, more
It fell down.
The cat ate the fish.

Natalie Boal (9)
St Oswald's Knuzden CE Primary School, Blackburn

SPRING CLEANING

One day I was spring cleaning,
When a little mouse ran out.
You should have seen the kerfuffle,
You should have heard me shout!
Grandma screaming,
Grandad dreaming,
Auntie Dot crying,
Uncle Sid lying,
The dog howling,
The baby scowling,
Mum moaning,
Dad groaning.
My sister jumped on a chair,
The cat was chasing the mouse,
The dog was chasing the cat . . .
And there I am stuck in the middle of that!

Laura Hartley (9)
St Oswald's Knuzden CE Primary School, Blackburn

FIREWORKS

The Roman candle goes hiss
Like an angry snake.
The Red Dragon goes *bang, bang, bang*
like a giant drum.
Whoosh! goes the Catherine wheel
like a shooting star.
Crack! goes the sparkler
like a crackling fire.
The rocket goes *boom!*
like a stick of dynamite.

Lewis Devine (9)
St Oswald's Knuzden CE Primary School, Blackburn

My Cousin

My cousin screams and screams,
Then she eats some pears.
After that she scatters around,
Then I give her a pound.

She asked me for something to eat,
So I gave her a little sweet.
Then she stayed for tea
And all she left was a pea.

Niall Taylor (8)
St Oswald's Knuzden CE Primary School, Blackburn

Roller Coaster

Roller coaster, roller coaster, take me up high,
Roller coaster, roller coaster, up in the sky.
With a spark at the back,
I'm sure you won't lack,
With a bar across my face,
I'm sure it will be ace,
I sure wish I was older,
With my dad's hand on my shoulder.

Ryan Hammond (8)
St Oswald's Knuzden CE Primary School, Blackburn

The Funfair

Me, my mum and my gran,
Are going to the fair,
We're going to go on a roller coaster,
I hope it won't mess up my hair!

We're going to go on the tea cups,
We're going to whizz round and round,
But when we get off the ride,
I'll probably fall to the ground.

Hannah Rawcliffe (9)
St Oswald's Knuzden CE Primary School, Blackburn

BONFIRE NIGHT

Bonfire Night! I love it!
Your sparkly sparks,
Rockets banging in the silent sky.
The fire's flames, wiggly, waggly,
Screamers, loud, noisy, annoying,
Hurting my ears.
Fast turning Catherine wheel,
Spinning faster than a car's wheels.

Shauna Chambers (8)
St Oswald's Knuzden CE Primary School, Blackburn

NOISE

I pay my money at the counter
As I walk through the door
Then I make my way through the crowd
Then I say, 'Oh my, that's Amy.'

Then I go back through the crowd
To see people singing out loud
To see people laughing
Crying, playing, eating.

Yazmin Gilbert (8)
St Oswald's Knuzden CE Primary School, Blackburn

THE CONCERT

I'm going to a concert,
With my auntie and my mum,
We're going to get some popcorn
To fill my hungry tum.

I'm getting ready in my seat,
I'm really, really excited,
I'm ready to dance to the beat,
I'm really, really delighted.

There is a tremendous noise,
There are screaming girls and boys,
I've got a headband that lights up,
I'm sipping Coke from my cup.

Alana McNulty (8)
St Oswald's Knuzden CE Primary School, Blackburn

THE ZOO

The zoo is so noisy
It makes me laugh
I like to watch the monkeys dance in hats
The lions roar like a man in pain
I like to hear the elephants trumpeting
Gorillas beat their chests
Like a band playing drums
I like to tease the tigers by pulling faces.

Kurt Sumner (8)
St Oswald's Knuzden CE Primary School, Blackburn

NAUGHTY GIRLS

'Stop that!' screamed Mum
'Stop that!' said Dad
'Don't be so nasty
and so bad!'

'Stop shouting you lot!
You're getting on my nerves!
When I get angry
I'll give you the scares!'

'Go to your room
You horrible girls,
Or I'll get your things
And those silly plastic pearls!'

'It's her fault you know
And they're actually mine,
I'm using them for my dolly
To make it shine.'

'Well, I need them more
I'm dressing myself up,
I'm playing party
And they match my tea cup.'

'Now I own up
It's got to be hers,
But now I'm hungry
Can I have some pears?'

Jane Baxter (8)
St Oswald's Knuzden CE Primary School, Blackburn

FIREWORKS TONIGHT

Rockets, screamers, bangers,
Catherine wheels lurching around in the sky.
Everybody screaming as fireworks go by.
I hold a sparkler in my hand and wave it all around
As I watch the sparks fall to the ground.

Lauren Orr (9)
St Oswald's Knuzden CE Primary School, Blackburn

HENRY VIII

Henry was a king.
He had six wives.
He didn't like to sing.
The first five wives tried to save their lives.
Wives 2 and 5's heads went *ping!*
He didn't chop them off with carving knives.
He only wanted a son to be king.

Chelsey Mawman (9)
St Oswald's Knuzden CE Primary School, Blackburn

MY BABY COUSIN

My baby cousin can almost say my name,
But it doesn't sound quite the same.
She can use a potty well,
Oh no, she's just fell.
I took her to beddy-bows,
She has got a blocked nose.

Amy Slater (8)
St Oswald's Knuzden CE Primary School, Blackburn

THE NEW HEAD TEACHER

The new head teacher was as thin as a pin,
But she was as smelly as a rubbish bin.
Her voice was really, really loud
And she's always looking very proud.
She is never happy, but very strict,
Until one day her pencil was nicked.
She always writes, can't you see
And she never stops for a cup of tea.
Her hair is short and very black
And then one day she got the sack.

One really bright and sunny day,
As most people would actually say,
We had a spelling test to do,
But then I heard someone shout, 'Aye, you.'
I looked outside to see who was there,
It was the head teacher shouting at a boy with a nit in his hair.
Her solicitor was there at the same time,
He said she is like a poem that doesn't rhyme.
He said that she makes him feel sick,
Then she said that he's taking the mick.

She was really upset at what her solicitor said
And then her face started to turn red.
Her solicitor gave her the sack,
Then a boy ran outside and his name was Jack.
Jack went to see the head teacher
And said, 'Would you like a slice of pizza?'
Her solicitor was really proud,
To see the head teacher crying out loud.
Jack was crying for she was his mum,
Jack couldn't believe the solicitor thought his mum was dumb.
The moral of this poem is,
Never sack a head teacher who shouted at a boy with a nit.

Adam Gough (9)
St Theresa's RC Primary School, Chester

THE NEW BOY

A new boy joined our school.
He is really shy but he thinks he's cool.
His name is Paddy.
Everyone calls him Fatty.
He has spots on his face
And he wears an old brace.
His hair is like chips in a pan
And he has a really bad tan.

Paddy is at St Theresa's School
And thinks he is really cool.
Paddy wears a mouldy old brace
And has spots on his face.
Everyone calls him Fatty,
You should see his daddy.

One day I saw Paddy in the street,
With no shoes on his feet.
Paddy likes going outside
And going for a ride.

One day I saw Paddy by the school
And he said, 'I am really cool.'
Paddy likes playing with sand
And Paddy writes with his right hand.

All the Year 6s bully Paddy
And call him Fatty.
All the Year 6s are really bad
And that makes me sad.

Stacey Thompson (10)
St Theresa's RC Primary School, Chester

THE NEW BOY

A new boy came to our school called Paddy,
He was a bit of a fatty.
Paddy has a blackening smile
That you can even see for a mile.
Never mind about his waxy ears,
Paddy's hair is as spiky as spears.
Now his hairy eyebrows are as round as a bridge,
Now really, if you want to see him,
He'll be in the fridge.

In class one day Paddy sat,
Paddy got bored and decided to sound like a cat.
The bell rang for break and Paddy went, 'Yes!'
Paddy ran around the class making an untidy mess.

Five years on, Paddy was in class,
Slurping water out of a glass.
Along came five children while Paddy was doing his work
And gave poor Paddy a horrible smirk.

Ten years later, Paddy was walking down the street,
Eating a box of something sweet.
Some mean men marched down the road
And battered poor Paddy to the size of a toad.

The moral of this poem is -
Don't judge a person by the way they look
And then just batter them.

Emily Boyne (9)
St Theresa's RC Primary School, Chester

PADDY DOWELL THE TRAMP

One day I saw Paddy by the riverside,
He had big ears with yellow wax inside.
He had greasy brown hair,
Which stunk like a bear.
He had long fingernails,
As long as dogs' tails.
His teeth were black like his mum's coal sack,
He had spots on his face and a rotten brace.

One early morning I went for a walk up by the river,
I saw Paddy having a bath,
I thought it was a little laugh.
So I came back the next day,
It looked like he had run away.
So he was gone for the rest of the years,
I'm sure I won't shed any tears.

Shaun Arathoon (9)
St Theresa's RC Primary School, Chester

THE HALF MAN

The moon was like a piece of round cheese tossed into the clear sky.
The wind was like a bull charging for miles around with its horns
                                          sticking up high.
The path was like a rock smashed into tiny pieces and there stood
                                          the half man staring, staring.

The half man is half-man, half-beast,
I think he wants us for a feast.
He has horrible red, glowing eyes,
He tells loads of lies.
He has razor-sharp claws,
But if you think they are sharp, his toenails are like saws.

But one night he had a rough time,
So in the night he woke up in fright.
There was a gun pointed at his head and
Bang! He was dead.

Nicholas Foster (10)
St Theresa's RC Primary School, Chester

PADDY DOWELL THE BULLY OF YEAR 5

One day a new boy came to our school, his name was Paddy,
Lots of cruel children called him Fatty.
He had spots all over his dirty face
And one disgusting, blinding brace.
Teachers thought that Paddy should do well,
But he is that naughty, he isn't allowed in the dell.
Paddy thought that he was cool,
He thought he could rock the school.

Paddy walked into the class,
He was that mad, he even broke a piece of glass.
He beat up one of the children for a stupid reason,
This happened in the middle of the summer season.
He beat him up because he got the tiniest bit of mud on his coat,
The coat he wears to go on a boat.

Paddy started to feel threatened,
His enemies came up to Paddy acting like a legend.
A bully came up to Paddy to get him back,
Just while one of the teachers was getting the sack.
Now Paddy has been taught a lesson,
In the end Paddy turned out to have a wonderful session.

The lesson is that you don't go bullying children
For doing the tiniest things wrong.

Jessica Withington (9)
St Theresa's RC Primary School, Chester

THE NEW CLASS

One day a class came into school,
They all thought that they looked really cool.
But the teacher said, 'What happened to you?'
Then she shouted, 'What am I going to do?'
You should have seen what they looked like!
'Do I look alright?' said Mike.
'If you looked good, I wouldn't be mad.
To tell you the truth, you all look bad.'

When the children were on their way home,
One of them said, 'How will I look good?
I don't have a comb!'
So the next morning when they got to school,
They all said, 'Miss, that was really cruel.'
The teacher said, 'You should be thanking me
For what I've done.'
'No I shouldn't. Everyone's laughing,
Even my mum.'
One of the children said, 'We have to fix this mess.'
Then another one said, 'I know. It's bad enough
She's making the girls wear a dress.'

At break the children didn't know what to do
And when they got in from break
The teacher said, 'I'm not being cruel to you.'
When they went to the dinner hall for lunch,
You wouldn't have heard a munch.
For a while when they were at school,
They thought that they would be really cruel.
I think it was the teacher that made them so mad,
Why they decided to be bad.
The moral of this poem is -
Never judge a book by how it looks.

James Graham (9)
St Theresa's RC Primary School, Chester

A POEM ABOUT PADDY DOWELL

Today a new boy started our school,
We all thought he was really cool,
Until we found that he was a fool.
He had a face like a pizza base
And a horrible black and white brace.
He was so dumb, he could not do a sum
And then he decided to hum.
But he was so fat he hadn't got a friend
Because they all thought he was a hen.
But then one day he changed his life,
He said, 'I'll go on a diet to get as thin as a knife.'
He said, 'I'll cut down on the chocolate bars,'
Then no one thought he was from Mars.
The moral of this poem is -
Don't judge people by the way they look.

Danielle Clutton (9)
St Theresa's RC Primary School, Chester

YELLOW!

Yellow is sunflowers swaying in the breeze,
Yellow is my sister's hair swishing down her back,
Yellow is the sky when the sun has just gone down,
Yellow is a lemon that has just been picked,
Yellow is the feeling you get when you're happy,
Yellow is cabbage when it has been boiled too much,
Yellow is the glisten of a sharp, silver needle,
Yellow is the gleam of the sun under your chin when you like butter,
Yellow is the gleam of sherbet just about to be eaten,
Yellow is the puff of popcorn in the tub.

Ruth Kirk (9)
Statham CP School, Lymm

What Is Sadness?

It's that fight with your friend
that makes you want to cry.

It's the moment in time
when someone you care for must die.

When hatred takes over
when you think you will be lonely forever.

Thinking of someone you've never seen
or will see.

But no matter how sad you are
you know that's the way things must be.

And it's when you are separated
from someone you admire.

No one should suffer in these ways.

Rebecca Cuffe (9)
Statham CP School, Lymm

Yellow

Yellow is the colour of Robinsons orange fruit juice,
    at the ready to quench your thirst.
Yellow is the colour of the fire alarm on the wall,
    ready to warn you of the heat.
Yellow is the colour that tells you to warm up,
Yellow is the colour of the dog next door,
Yellow is the colour of the lightning in the sky.

Peter Booth (9)
Statham CP School, Lymm

ICICLE

A
shimmering
icicle.
Is
that
what
I
see
sparkling
in
the
warm
sunlight?

Kate Kirkwood (9)
Statham CP School, Lymm

GRANDAD

I stand before him, lying in the wet damp soil,
One more teardrop fell from my eye.
I can only remember eight years ago
It dropped from beneath the clouds.
As I stood there, one last teardrop fell from my eye.
I cry for his death.
I will never speak of it again.
As one last teardrop fell from my eye.
In my room I sat and sat there.
Then I stood and I saw a rainbow.
I cannot speak of anything so sad again.
As one last teardrop fell from my eye.

Rachel Jones (9)
Statham CP School, Lymm

MY DREAM

I look around,
See lilac walls
And then it happens.
My heart suddenly falls
At the sight of this wonderful masterpiece
And cute animals galore.
Then I look down,
See the floor,
Purple, I think with glee
And then I think
How does this happen to me?
I close my eyes,
Open them again
And then I see,
It's not a dream at all.
I think how lucky I must be,
To have a bedroom like thee.

Victoria Copley (9)
Statham CP School, Lymm

RED IS LIKE THE SETTING SUN

Red is like the setting sun
Red is like you've just won
Red shines as the burning sky
Still nobody knows why
Red is the colour of burning fire
Red is the colour I admire
Red is also my desire
Red is a useful colour
It is the taste of Müller!

Joseph Broadsmith (9)
Statham CP School, Lymm

LOLLIPOP

Once I saw a lollipop
In the window of a shop
The price said boldly '25p'
Then I shouted loudly, 'Mummy!'
After moaning for half an hour
She had to give in before I shouted louder

Once I saw a lollipop
In the window of a shop
The bright orange, juicy one
Get it now before it's gone
Imagine licking that gleaming thing
If it goes then there'll be none

Once I saw a lollipop
In the window of a shop
Looks too lovely to resist
If the lady won't give it to me
I will give her my fist!

Josh Boyle (9)
Statham CP School, Lymm

HOLIDAY

Once upon a butterfly,
Up above the clouds go by,
The sun is shining on me,
As I watch a bumblebee,
I take a dip in the pool,
The water is nice and cool,
Once upon a butterfly,
Now my holiday has gone by.

Jamie Johnson (10)
Statham CP School, Lymm

WINTER

Winter is the time of year,
When people hear,
The jingle jangle of the bells,
While waiting in the cells.

They're waiting for St Nick,
They don't want to pick,
For they are waiting silently,
For him to finally arrive.

They hear the jingle on the roof,
Some may be asleep on the pouffe,
He goes around very quickly,
Even though some are sickly,
He goes to each house,
Moving like a mouse.

If you are good,
Then he just could,
Come to your house,
Creeping like a mouse
And under your tree,
You might see,
Some little presents,
Just for you!

Hannah Blackwell (10)
Statham CP School, Lymm

ME (HAIKU)

My name is Sophie,
People around me are kind,
We help each other.

Sophie Blackwell (8)
Statham CP School, Lymm

KEIRAN

His smile is like a grinning crocodile,
His laugh is like a boom box with a CD in it,
He chatters like a monkey,
He swims like a goldfish.

Joseph Artine (8)
Statham CP School, Lymm

BLUE

Blue is like the clear sky,
Blue is like the clear, deep sea,
Blue is like the clear, fresh pool,
Blue is like you are frozen,
Blue is like the deep, cold ocean,
Blue is like a jacuzzi bubbling,
Blue is like a fresh blueberry,
Blue is like an icy Christmas Day,
Blue is like a blue pansy.

Nicola Richards (9)
Statham CP School, Lymm

HAIKU

My name is Alan.
I am too poor to buy food.
I live on the streets.

Kieran Crow (9)
Statham CP School, Lymm

A Day At School

Time to work and have lots of fun
The school day has just begun
Come on, wake up, yes I mean you
Whichever class you're in, there's loads to do
Whatever your interests from PE to English
There are play times each day to do as you wish
Then it's all over, time to go home
And then there's lots of homework over which you can moan!

Katy Burgess (10)
Statham CP School, Lymm

My Bike

Wind is in my face,
Pedals spinning very fast,
Spokes spinning, going crazy.

Sam Brennan (9)
Statham CP School, Lymm

Playing For Wolverhampton AFC

The sun turning, as the crowd cheers around the ground.
My first goal had come,
Playing for Wolverhampton AFC.

Ryan Green (8)
Statham CP School, Lymm

SNOW

As snow floats from the sky
Excitement rushes past me inside
Snowflakes fall onto my window
I wonder what it will be like tomorrow

The clouds are high
The morning is nigh
I look out of my window
And a wonderful sight meets my eyes

For hours and hours I would play
In the snow that's where I'd stay
Until it all melts.

Sarah Hargreaves (10)
Statham CP School, Lymm

GRABBING ATTENTION

Watch out, watch out, you'd better beware,
The teachers come to stand and stare.
No time to chat or look away,
You're at school now and here to stay.

It's time to learn all sorts of things,
To help you spread your learning wings.
So buckle up and get to work,
It's not as bad as you first thought.

Paul Hackett (10)
Statham CP School, Lymm

MY HOLIDAY

The plane went on time
And a window to see,
Then a lady with tea
And a little treat for me,
Our landing was jerky,
Then our luggage to get,
We collect our car
And we are all set.

We find our way,
Past large fields and trees
And farmers with horses,
Look so at ease,
We find our hotel,
It all looks so grand,
So sunny and warm
And look, there's the sand.

Down to the beach,
For some lovely ice cream,
Then up to the surf,
Is it a dream?
I swim for a while
And jump over waves,
And look over there,
Some dark-looking caves.

We'll go inland tomorrow,
So much to learn,
But soon it's all over,
It's time to return.

Kameel Somani (10)
Styal Primary School, Wilmslow

IF I COULD PAINT THE IMPOSSIBLE . . .

If I could paint impossible sounds, they would be
Gigantic crowds, cheering wildly for you,
Someone you deeply respect saying,
'Well done. You did that perfectly.'
The sound of a hot bath running just for you,
As if the person who ran it knew that you had had a bad day.
But the most impossible sound of all would be
The brilliant sound of life.

If I could paint impossible movements, they would be
The people of the world all living in harmony,
With no disputes or wars,
A lark flying freely in a mountain range, singing sweetly,
People enjoying their lives, making decisions for themselves,
But the most impossible movement of all would be
The poor, sick children in Brazil
Running around with no illness or poverty,
Living life to the maximum.

If I could paint impossible smells, they would be
The luscious smell of your little brother's or sister's pudding
Wafting up your nose,
After you've discovered that you don't like your own,
The angelic smell of your favourite pudding
When you're eating your greens,
The greasy smell of a modern restaurant
When your parents have taken you to an old-fashioned one
That smells all musty, like a church,
But the most impossible smell of all would be
The smell of your dad's Chinese spare ribs when you're in bed.

George Massey (10)
Styal Primary School, Wilmslow

MY UNCLE ZACKARY

My Uncle Zackary Custardworth-Hoast,
Seems to believe that he is a ghost.
He lives in a cupboard under the stairs
And spooks people out at the haunted house fairs.

When the clock strikes twelve each and every night,
He jumps out of the cupboard and gives us a fright.
He lurks in the shadows and creeps round the corners,
He makes us all leap and gives us the horrors.

When my Uncle Zackary dressed up for dinner,
He looked like something that came straight from 'Thriller'.
The deep purple suit that was covered in dust,
With six shiny buttons that had started to rust.

On his 40th birthday everyone left,
He fell asleep in his pudding and it stuck on his chest.
As he ran through a wall and knocked himself out,
We thought that's not clever without any doubt.

When Uncle Zackary was trying to hover,
He jumped off the table and yelled, 'Bother, bother.
What is the point of being a ghost,
When you can't walk through walls and you can't fly and float?'

I said, 'Uncle Zack, why don't you drop it?
You can't be a ghost, so you might as well stop it.'
He replied, 'Don't be silly, you know I'm a ghoul.'
I said, 'You're behaving just like a fool.'

Uncle Zackary said, 'I know I'm a fool,
But playing a ghost is really quite cool.
I can't walk through walls or take off my head,'
Then he rose from the floor and floated to bed!

Heather Talbot (11)
Styal Primary School, Wilmslow

THE GIRAFFE AND THE HIPPO

There was a giraffe
Who had such a laugh
When a hippo decided to dance
He put on a skirt
With a little pink shirt
And funny, bright yellow pants.

Beat after beat
He danced for a treat
But never once won a medal
Giraffe said, 'Hey ho
You're going too slow
Perhaps you ought to pedal.'

So he got on a bike
And went for a hike
But didn't get very far
Before he could stop
He fell - *plop, plop, plop*
And landed in a heap of black tar.

He slowly got up
And brushed himself down
Then made the slow trip to town
He looked at giraffe
Who now didn't laugh
As he passed in the car
To see his poor friend covered in tar.

Sam Dixon (10)
Styal Primary School, Wilmslow

The Carousel

I've nearly finished my breakfast and dawn
has arrived
I'm off to the fairground to the fantastic
carousel
Walking over the cobbles I hear the laughter of
children
Sixpence clasped in hand waiting to pay my
fare
The driver takes my sixpence and puts me on
a horse
Up and down I go, bobbing along on the dobby
horse
When my ride is over - I make my way back
home
Tired and sleepy
I climb into bed dreaming of the next time the
fair is in town.

Oliver Bayne (10)
Styal Primary School, Wilmslow

Friends

I used to feel so lonely
Until my grandma said,
'What you need is a special pet,
to be your special friend.'

First I got a goldfish who swam about a lot,
Then I got a hamster, a guinea pig and a frog.
Next I got a mouse,
A rabbit and a dog.

Now I'm not so lonely
Cos I'm busy all the time,
Our house is full of pets
And Grandma thinks it's fine.

James Morgan (10)
Styal Primary School, Wilmslow

FEELINGS

Freedom is the taste of fresh air and juicy fresh fruit.
The smell of green trees and newly cut grass.
The sound of birds singing and bees buzzing.
It feels like soft grass and cold, fresh air.
Finally, freedom is the colour of the light blue sky
And dark green grass.

Danger is the smell of death and damp, wet walls.
The sound of screams and shouting.
It feels like spikes and very rough prickles.
It tastes like poison and rotten milk.
It looks like hot fire and dripping red blood.
Finally, danger is the colour dark red and pitch-black.

Hope is the taste of sweet strawberries and cream.
The sound of music and laughter.
It feels like soft silk and fluffy white rabbits.
It smells like lilies and roses.
It looks like the sun shining and fluffy white clouds.
Finally, hope is the colour of light pink and navy blue.

Hannah Jagger (10)
Styal Primary School, Wilmslow

IF I COULD PAINT . . .

If I could paint . . .
Impossible movements they would be
Planets spinning around in space,
The sea trickling up the beach,
Palm trees on a windy day
And horses' hooves galloping swiftly.

If I could paint . . .
Impossible smells they would be
The smell of leftover coffee,
Mum's home-made chocolate cake,
Fresh, juicy, ripe cherries
And thick, crispy bacon.

If I could paint . . .
Impossible colours they would be
The faint blue ocean flowing rapidly,
Red pouring blood,
My dim, black shadow
And a pale yellow daffodil growing from the ground.

Hannah Bate (10)
Styal Primary School, Wilmslow

STORM

When I lie in bed,
Looking at the sunless sky,
It is as jet-black as a raven bird.
My eyes opened suddenly, midnight -
Crash! No silence,
But the sound of the fierce sea
Crashing on the rocks.

Looking out of the window
At the dark, dingy sea,
Sleepless on my rocking chair,
Reading spooky stories,
My little, round, fluffy cat
Hiding under my arm.

Paige Watkinson (10)
Styal Primary School, Wilmslow

IF I COULD PAINT . . .

Incredible movements they would be . . .
The branches swaying in the wind of a summer's day
The waves crashing against a rocky shore
A child rocking up and down on his chair
and nearly falling off
The sun setting beyond the horizon

Amazing sounds they would be . . .
People laughing and having a good time
A bird singing merrily in a large oak tree
The roar of an aeroplane taking off
The beat of a drum being hit in a rock band

Impossible colours they would be . . .
All the colours of the rainbow that will light up
the darkest room
A rich purple that looks warm and welcoming
A blood-red that makes people feel happy inside.

Benjamin Hyde (11)
Styal Primary School, Wilmslow

THE WAY THROUGH THE WOODS

They shut the road through the woods
Ninety years ago.
Rain and snow have undone again
And now you would never know
There was once a road through the woods
Before they planted the trees.
It is underneath the coppice and heath
And the thin daisies.
Only the keeper sees
That, where the ring robin broods
And the foxes tiptoe at ease,
There was once a road through the woods.
Yet, if you enter the woods
Of a winter morning late,
When the morning air - cooling on the trout-ringed pools
Where the fish swims to his mate
(They fear not hunters because they see so few),
You will hear the beat of a rabbit's feet
And a swish of a tail in the dew,
Steadily jumping through
The misty solitudes,
As though they perfectly knew
The old lost road through the woods . . .
But there is no road through the woods!

Naomi Tetler (10)
Styal Primary School, Wilmslow